Understanding
Demonic Strategies

KEYS TO DECODING
SATAN'S STRATEGIC PLAN

Roosevelt Ethridge

Understanding Demonic Strategies: Keys to Decoding Satan's Strategic Plan

by Roosevelt Ethridge, Jr.

Published by ReziPrint, LLC.

Rezolucian Image and Design House LLC.

PO Box 981

Wilson, North Carolina 27894

www.reziprint.com

This book or parts thereof may not be reproduced in any form, stored in a retrieval system, or transmitted in any form by any means—electronic, mechanical, photocopy, recording, or otherwise—without prior written permission of the publisher, except as provided by United States of America copyright law.

Unless otherwise noted, all Scripture quotations are from the King James Version of the Bible. Scripture quotations marked NKJV are taken from the New King James Version®. Copyright © 1982 by Thomas Nelson. Used by permission. All rights reserved.

Cover design by Kendra N. Sumler for Aesthetic Mentality

Ccover Author photo by Dante Lucas for DLucas Photography

Edited by Daniel Ruff for T's and I's, Inc.

Copyright © 2022 by Roosevelt Ethridge, Jr.

All rights reserved.

Visit the author's website: https://www.reliveglobalcorp.com.

International Standard Book Number: 979-8-98663270-5-1

While the author has made every effort to provide accurate telephone numbers and Internet addresses at the time of publication, neither the publisher nor the author assumes any responsibility for errors or for changes that occur after publication.

First edition

Printed in the United States of America

To those who continue to fight the good fight of faith--- being relentless, content, and faithful until His return.

~ Global Leader

Table of Contents

Introduction VI
Demonic Strategies 9
Satan's ID 25
Devil Strategic Plan 37
Satan's Military Organizational Structure 47
Military Infrastructure of the Devil's Kingdom 56
Rules of Engagement 64
Demonic Concepts of War 71
Strategies of War 79
Artillery and Weapons 91
Kingdom Intelligence 97
SELECTED BIBLIOGRAPHY 101
Notes 103

Introduction

Understanding Demonic Strategies

[1] Blessed *is* the man
Who walks not in the counsel of the ungodly,
Nor stands in the path of sinners,
Nor sits in the seat of the scornful;
[2] But his delight *is* in the law of the LORD,
And in His law he meditates day and night

Psalm 1

For centuries, Satan has been challenging the church. He has orchestrated an organized kingdom that he uses to carry out his plans, and his schemes. Throughout history, the church has been known for to fighting spiritual battles, witchcraft, and powers of darkness. In the New Testament, Paul uses a lot of symbolism to convey the battles between the dark world and mankind.

There are many people who have found it challenging to discover demonic strategies and dispel them. Satan's strategies can be complex, in some cases very simplistic. The theory of Satan ruling the world is real to some people, but it should not be the truth of the believer. It is Satan's desire that believers lose credibility in the manifested power of God. It has been implied to some believers to minimize their acknowledgement of the devil because he only has the power that you give him.

It is important that we can identify Satan and the plots of his hand. His strategic plan involves him manipulating people to discredit the work of the cross and denied the redemptive power of God through Jesus Christ. Therefore, to keep his agenda progressing forward, Satan uses a structured government. There are some Satanic communities that classify Satan as the High Priest. This terminology should not frighten the believer, in the book of Revelation, we are able to read about the war in the heavens and how Satan was banished to the earth. In order to keep his agenda fervent, he used manipulation and persuasion to convince a third of the heaven to believe in his plot.

In his organizational chart, Satan is the head of his army. The devil is the one who releases the command for communities, families, and individuals to be attacked. He will create unforeseen challenges and difficulties causing mankind to remain at war with each other. Satan also uses money and people in the earth to monopolize, control, and dominate regions.

However, knowing how the dark world is structured can give opportunity for believers in the earth to triumph, have victory, and advance the enemy. Satan understands that if people deny the existence of Jesus Christ and the redemptive work of the cross, that he has a chance to keep people from sharing the love of Jesus Christ.

This book is a manual that can be used like a textbook to study the character of Satan in a modern world. The author provides great things live the 'Rules of Engagement', and 'Kingdom Intelligence' to provide insight to believers of war. Walking through the chapters of this book can assist the reader in gaining a new perspective on spiritual battles and engaging in war at ground zero. *Understanding Demonic Strategies* can be used simultaneously will studying areas of spiritual warfare against the enemy.

1
Demonic Strategies

¹I will extol You, O Lord, for You have lifted me up,
And have not let my foes rejoice over me.
² O Lord my God, I cried out to You,
And You healed me.
³ O Lord, You brought my soul up from the grave;
You have kept me alive, [a]that I should not go down to the pit.

Psalm 30

In war, concept and strategies are considered for armies engage in battle. There is much deliberation when planning for a war. Top officials talk about when the battle should begin, where the battle will take place. Officials also discuss the strength and knowledge of the other army. Declaring war on another army is by the commander-in-chief of the army. In today's time, war is engaged when powers break the rules of war or certain sects are rising as independent powers terrorizing their people and others.

Satan engages war against the believer without adhering to any rules of engagement. Spiritual battles are not like battles in the natural, however, natural battles can be heavily influenced by evil. When men give themselves over to evil intentions, they become capable of employing immoral behaviors in the earth. In the *City of God* Saint Augustine says,

"But the devils, whom these men repute gods, are content that even iniquities they are guiltless of should be ascribed to them, so long as they may entangle men's minds in the meshes of these opinions, and draw them on along with themselves to their predestinated punishment: whether such things were actually committed by the men whom these devils, delighting in human infatuation, caused to be worshipped as gods, and in whose stead they, by a thousand malign and deceitful artifices, substitute themselves, and so receive worship; or whether, though they were really the crimes of men, these wicked spirits gladly allowed them to be attributed to higher beings that there might seem to be conveyed from heaven itself a sufficient sanction for the perpetration of shameful wickedness."[1]

In spiritual battles, the devil predetermines your response by using a calculated process that involves your thoughts, feelings, and reality. The strategic plan in spiritual warfare initiated by the devil comes from Satan himself. Satan does not consult with a council to strategize against a person, community, or country. In Saint Augustine's response in *City of God,* one of the strategies that the enemy is employing currently is a combination of idolatry and self-gratification techniques.

Strategically calculated, Satan knows if any person would engage in this manner that they would eventually self-destruct. This destruction would be a by-product of one entertaining vices. The next chapter will detail the cause and effect of 'vices.' However, it is important to note that the strategizing is an attribute of the Enemy. Yes, God will give you strategy but do not overlook the fact that many traumatic and unexpected disturbances that you experience are pre-calculated strategies that the Enemy has created against you.

Before Satan was banished from Heaven he served in the council of God. We see this exemplified in the Book of Job when, Satan and God have an exchange during his appearance amongst the heavenly council. In contemporary Christian settings it is hard for many to believe that Satan was not evil in Job. When we see these terms: devil, Satan, or serpent read in scripture and used interchangeably when assessing demonic manifestations attributed to evil works. In Genesis 3 when the woman converses with the serpent and Job 1 are exceptions. Mitchell Reddish says, "In Job, the word "Satan" is not a proper noun. It is descriptive rather than nominative. In Hebrew, "Satan" means "the adversary" or "the accuser." In Job, "Satan" plays the role of the heavenly informer and tester of people's faithfulness to God."[2] Even though Satan was part of the heavenly council during this time, when he was removed from the heavens, he kept the skills and attributes gained from being trained amongst the council.

Character Assassination

Uniformly many Christians associate the devil with being a musician primarily. Therefore, they relate music are his primary use, yet in keeping with the theme of this writing, we understand Satan is a strategist and will work diligently, far outside the bounds of 'improper music infiltration'. Character assassination is a great ploy used by the enemy as demonstrated in Job 1. Satan employs several strategies against Job with the intent to get him to recant his commitment to God. In Job 1 v. 11, "But now, stretch out Your hand and touch all that he has, and he will surely curse You to Your face!" Satan used a strategy with God to blemish Jobs character in God. Since being removed from the heavens, Satan does not employ this method against God, but he will employ it against the believer. He uses this strategy to get the individual to discredit themselves in areas of life where God has appointed them.

David and Janice decided it was time for them to move to another location. For the past 15 years they have lived as a two-income household. One day David felt led by the Lord that it was time for them to move to another city. However, Janice was not at peace with the decision because they had just recently gained some comfort and normalcy in their lives with finance and stability. After having more conversation, they joined together to trust God with their relocation. The move was successful! They both were blessed and rejoicing in the Lord. Unexpectedly after being in the new location for 3 weeks, David was laid-off from the new job. With all of their faith in God, the Enemy used the lay-off as a way to challenge their character in God. The Enemy challenged them psychological about their timing and their feelings. They both trusted God for the move but immediately became disturbed in God by the unexpected lay-off. When the Enemy is after your character, he initiates an internal war within yourself that can invite outward negative criticism about your decision-making ability.

Financial Assassination

Job was affected by Satan's tactic of financial assassination as well. This is demonstrated in Chapter 1 when his entire lively hood is obliterated. Creating financial challenge is a strategy that the Enemy uses often to diminish the believer's trust in God's ability to provide in their situation. The financial challenge strategy can confuse the believer or place them in immediate hardship, which can lead the believer to trust in their own abilities. Proverbs 3 vs. 5-6 says, "Trust in the Lord with all your heart, and lean not on your own understanding; In all your ways acknowledge Him, And He shall direct your paths." Defeating the Enemy in financial challenges require focus and should include determination so that you can have the ability to focus on the big picture which is God. Secondarily, do not allow downsizing, budgeting, and living a restricted lifestyle to frustrate your financial recovery.

In the example earlier with David and Janice, when David was laid off by his employer, it immediately changed their circumstances but not their God. Job suffers great loss that confuses everyone that knows he is a great manager of money and resources. This strategy of the devil is potent, he can use this strategy to break-up homes, businesses, families, relationships, communities, ministries and more. There are times when the Enemy can use financial challenge to discredit your message as a minister of the gospel.

These areas of life can become challenged when one's economic security is troubled. In each area, Satan strategically calculates how his is going to deceive individuals and communities using finance as a weapon. Amongst finance, Satan attacks: family, health, marriages, and one's confidence. He does this by employing critiques and criticisms.

Family Annihilation

Job 1 vs. 18-19 says, "While he *was* still speaking, another also came and said, "Your sons and daughters *were* eating and drinking wine in their oldest brother's house, and suddenly a great wind came from across the wilderness and struck the four corners of the house, and it fell on the young people, and they are dead; and I alone have escaped to tell you!" When the Enemy employs this strategy, it is possible for a person to lose several family members by death, non-communication, or little to no support. When he is attacking the family, the attack could be to take a believer's attention and cause them to sabotage their destiny by deciding to no longer pursue their destiny.

Bobby Newton was thirty-five years old; he was married with two girls ages 5 and 9. One day in October of 1997 they all began their day as normal. Bobby would pray with his family just before leaving for work. Everything appeared to be going great, Bobby was excited about work because he was scheduled to meet with his boss about being promoted. On this day, around 2:00 PM Bobby received a phone call at work that changed his life forever. The local sheriff called him to tell him that his family had been in a fatal car accident. Bobby informed his boss and travelled to the location of his family. When Bobby arrived, he was told that no one in his family survived the accident. They were met on the road by a drunk driver who was two times over the legal limit for alcohol consumption. Bobby's life was shattered. For months he was burdened with the memory burying his entire family.

He was in pain because he never saw his daughters grow-up to be teenagers, he did not get to see them graduate or get married. Also, he felt robbed of not being able to grow old with his wife. For months, Bobby stopped living until he had a visitation by his wife in a dream. In the dream they conversed, and she encouraged Bobby to live. Bobby was frustrated with her suggesting this in the dream because his life was engulfed by their existence. In this situation Satan planned to kill the entire family. Even though Bobby was living, emotional pain and trauma took his life. He did not have a desire to dream or carry out any of the dreams he and his wife shared. After the angelic visitation with of his wife, through time he began to gain strength and life again. Just like in Job, Satan really believed in his heart that Job would stop trusting God when he initiated this strategy against his life.

Health Ambush

In Job chapter 2 Satan returned before the Lord. The Lord asked Satan, where you have been, have you tried my servant Job again since he held fast to his integrity in God with the other attacks,

Satan responded in vs. 4-5. He says, "So Satan answered the Lord and said, "Skin for skin! Yes, all that a man has he will give for his life. But stretch out Your hand now, and touch his bone and his flesh, and he will surely curse You to Your face!" Satan believed that Job would not remain committed to God if his health was attacked. There are times where Satan will ambush the health of the believer. It is possible for a person to experience unexpected health challenges or an unreasonable decline in health. Clive Staples Lewis (CS Lewis) describes this type of *health ambush* in his work called *The Screwtape Letters.* In his 6th letter to "Wormwood" he says,

> "There is nothing like suspense and anxiety for barricading a human's mind against the Enemy. He wants men to be concerned with what they do; our business is to keep them thinking about what will happen to them. Your patient will, of course, have picked up the notion that he must submit with patience to the Enemy's will. What the Enemy means by this is primarily that he should accept with patience the tribulation which has actually been dealt out to him---the present anxiety and suspense. --- It is your business to see that the patient never thinks of the present fear as his appointed cross, but only of the things he is afraid of. Let him regard them as his crosses: let him forget that, since they are incompatible, they cannot all happen to him, and let him try to practice fortitude and patience to them all in advance."[3]

Satan will use this attack against a person to with the intent of accomplishing several things with one battle. When believers or their loved ones are challenged in their body, Satan's agenda is to dismantle their belief in God, to discredit their profession, and to blind them from the healing power of God. The Enemy uses 'health ambushing' to cause onlookers to remain skeptical of the healing power of God. Not only does he employ this tactic to persuade the unbeliever, but he can use it to target the believer.

C.S. Lewis refers to two of the four *Cardinal Virtues* in his letter. He mentions fortitude and patience. We will talk more about these virtues later in this book. However, when the Enemy attacks the believer's health, it is common for him to also us psychological warfare simultaneously. How the Enemy perpetuates his strategic health plan against the believer is to cause the believer to discredit the function of medical science. The miracle power of God cannot be compared to the professional readiness of doctors, nurse practitioners, and other professionals in medicine. Therefore, the Enemy creates a conflict in the mind of the believer in some cases that mankind will disregard the function of medicine. So, with this disdain against medicine as we live in the age of the internet and self-diagnoses, many people use their own judgment in how to handle their sickness. The problem with this behavior is that some sicknesses are more severe than others.

In Job 2 v. 7 says, "So Satan went out from the presence of the Lord and struck Job with painful boils from the sole of his foot to the crown of his head." When Satan attacked Job's body, he was fully convinced that Job would give up on God. The enemy can use health challenges as a way to slow down the advancement of someone who is progressive. Making it of upmost importance for everyone to manage their recovery from sicknesses. As a person ages, their body responds differently in the recovery process as they battle sickness and disease. Practicing a healthy recovery method does not mean that the person is faithless. The bible says in Job 2 v. 8 that Job used a "potsherd" to scrape himself. This is important because the enemy thinks when he attacks the health of someone that they will not find comfort or relief. Healings can manifest in two forms, by way of medicine and by way of a supernatural manifestation. Satan does not want anyone to trust in the healing power of God when sickness befalls them. Matthew 10 v. 1 says, "And when He had called His twelve disciples to *Him,* He gave them power *over* unclean spirits, to cast them out, and to heal all kinds of sickness and all kinds of disease." The power to walk in healing after being attacked is doable.

Marriage Divide

The enemy will use a myriad of tactics to challenge marriages. Marriage requires couples to do intentional work to maintain a healthy relationship. In the Enemy's strategic plan, he attacks anything that perpetuates the covenant relationship that God has with man. Marriage is a union that will perpetuate this covenant relationship; therefore, the enemy will be intentional at creating a divide between couples. Adrian Rogers says, "According to the Word of God, the marriage relationship is a bond greater than that of parent and child, or child and parent: "Therefore shall a man leave his father and his mother and shall cleave unto his wife: and they shall be one flesh" (Gen. 2:24). According to this verse, there is no higher commitment---not business, position, or service."[4] Because of this level of commitment, the Devil does not make it easy for marriages to grow together.

In Job, the writer does not suggest how long that Job was married. However, we can assume that it was a long-time because of the age of his children at death. The eldest son had a house. Job's wife's name is not mentioned. However, her voice is heard in Job 2 v. 9. The Enemy uses her in this verse to initiate conflict within their marriage. After witnessing all of the loss that had become of Job, she asks a question that challenges his character in God. Job 2 v. 9 says, "Then his wife said to him, "Do you still hold fast to your integrity? Curse God and die!'" The Enemy will leverage his hand against a marriage when loss, financial challenge and struggle becomes part of the marriage lifestyle. This is not an implication to suggest that he makes marriage better just because a couple is financially fit. Dr. Henry Cloud and Dr. John Townsend says in their book, *Boundaries in Marriage,* "The marriage relationship is a covenant between two adults. They join lives to make a more meaningful and fruitful life together."[5]

The right conflict in a marriage can dismantle the marriage. The Enemy will use distrust or insecurity to unravel the love that two people have for each other. The distrust that marriages experience is not always connected to infidelity. However, there are many marriages that become challenged by the pressure that life adds to their relationship. Dr.'s Cloud and Townsend say,

> "Marriage is not designed to repair the brokenness of its partners, though it can certainly be a major healing agent. It is not designed to provide everything our families of origin did not. Nor is it designed to be the only place we go for comfort, help, truth, or growth. To be sole support for another person would put an impossible burden on each spouse."[6]

When a person has suffered pain throughout their life, it is possible for them to enter a marriage with unreasonable expectations. Moreover, being unreasonable in marital expectations can become a 'battle ground' for the Enemy. In Job 2 v. 9 it was unreasonable for Job's wife to expect him to curse God and give up on living. Based on God's account of Job in chapters 1 and 2, Job was devout and committed to him. When Job responds in v. 10, he is disappointed and frustrated in his wife. There are situations that the Enemy will create in a marriage to bring tension in hopes of ending that marriage. There are three primary areas in marriage that the enemy will use as his common areas for attack. The Enemy will use finance, communication, and commitment as his 'battle ground' of choice to attack marriages.

Out of the three, communication is a premium weapon he uses to destroy couples. Sometimes people assume that being together for a long-time implies that their communication towards each other is perfect. Unfortunately, this is not the truth. The enemy does not care how long people have been together as a couple as long as they are not able to comprehend, understand and forgive each other. When offense enters a marital union, it is like a grenade. Julian Perreira says, "A hand grenade is an anti-personnel weapon designed and used to clear out enemy fortifications, buildings or trenches. --- From pulling the pin and throwing a grenade, it usually takes anywhere between two to six seconds before detonation occurs."[7] When offense hit a marriage it is only a matter of seconds before that offense could become deadly for the couple's union. The Enemy chooses this method to get the couple working against each other. The greater the offense the greater the divide in some cases. Furthermore, the enemy strategically uses communication to further exacerbate the divide. He does this to engage in close combat warfare where emotional grenades are deployable.

Shirley Vinson says, "An offense is only as powerful as our reaction to it."[8] Marriages can avoid this strategy of the Enemy by being patient and forgiving with each other. In times of conflict, these are not times to quote scriptures or point out the fault in the other person. When conflicts arise, it is important to seek understanding about the conflict. Listening defensively will only cause a marriage to have a wedge in their union. Therefore, keeping love as the main thing and applying Christian ethics to every situation could help a couple survive the attacks of the Satan.

Critique and Criticism

Satan uses critique and criticism as automatic weapons during close combat. Negative critique from people that are respected can be used by the enemy as a pistol. The use of a pistol is not for long range targets; however, it can be uses to disengage a threat and offer a fatal shot that will disable a threat. Simultaneously he uses criticism as an automatic rifle. Shooting a rifle repetitively from a longer distance in order to disable potential or existing threats. We see this demonstrated in Job 2, when he is approached by his friends with critique and criticism about the loss he is experiencing in his life. The Enemy employs this tactic using a variety of ways. In addition to family, friends, business partners, associates, and even the internet.

Satan is fond of these weapons because the impact can destroy friendships, ministries, organizations, families, and individuals. When there is an imbalance between positive and negative criticism in a person's life, they can lose sight in their reason to succeed or even live. These weapons can control the thought and perception of mankind. Negative criticism can cloud the judgment of people. When a person has been dehumanized by critique, the enemy uses this to rob them of their own potential and opportunities. Carter G. Woodson said,

> "If you control a man's thinking you do not have to worry about his action. When you determine what a man shall think you do not have to concern yourself about what he will do. If you make a man feel that his is inferior, you do not have to compel him to accept an inferior status, for he will seek it himself. If you make a man think that he is justly an outcast, you do not have to order him to the back door. He will go without being told; and if there is no back door his very nature will demand one."[9]

This tactic that the Satan uses in not against one race of people. He uses this tactic against poverty-stricken mindsets. In Matthew 25 there is a parable of three men with talents. In this passage of scripture, the man with one talent does not do anything to multiply his talent. The opportunity was present for him to multiply but he chose to save the talent. When the Enemy engages these weapons against you, he is not intended for you to maximize your potential. He knows that too much negative critique will shut a person down who is not mentally fit to endure the battle of criticism.

Complaining, gossip and lying are like ammunition for these weapons. The Enemy energizes his fight by providing this type of ammo for the agents in his army. All of these thing's war against the soul of man. With this type of ammo Satan can create false accusations, stir up strife and create extreme competition amongst people. Romans 13 v. 13 says, "Let us walk properly, as in the day, not in revelry and drunkenness, not in lewdness and lust, not in strife and envy." The only order that the enemy submits to is the order of his kingdom. In his *strategic plan* he intends to make God's Kingdom chaotic. He challenges the moral order of society. Satan uses the same device of persuasion to influence mankind into not believing in what is right or wrong. More so, his plan encourages people to live life without restraints or discipline.

In the *Prince of Darkness,* Jeffrey Burton Russell mentions that philosophers traditionally argue there are three kinds of evil: moral, natural, and metaphysical.[10] The Enemy will attack in these areas to further excite confusion in the hearts of mankind. When Jesus was in the Mount of Olives, he taught his disciples about the signs of the end-times. Moreover, during this teaching, he is also giving the disciples the methodology of the Enemy they will face in the earth. Matthew

24 vs. 5-10 say,

> "For many will come in My name, saying, 'I am the Christ,' and will deceive many. And you will hear of wars and rumors of wars. See that you are not troubled; for all *these things* must come to pass, but the end is not yet. For nation will rise against nation, and kingdom against kingdom. And there will be famines, pestilences, and earthquakes in various places. All these *are* the beginning of sorrows. "Then they will deliver you up to tribulation and kill you, and you will be hated by all nations for My name's sake. And then many will be offended, will betray one another, and will hate one another."

The Enemy uses strategies and concepts because his kingdom is organized. His plans are damaging and destructive. There is nothing good that comes out of the Enemy's plan against mankind. Those who serve his agenda are the only ones that benefit from his plan. Derek Prince says, "But somewhere between God's heavenly domain and us is a hostile kingdom that opposes us and seeks to hinder our prayers. And that is why we sometimes have to push through the enemy territory when we pray."[11]

The devil comes after you because of your profession of Christ in your heart. He does not care if you have received salvation yesterday or if you have been a faithful servant for years, it is his desire to get as many people to fall prey to his plan. 1 Peter 5 v. 8 says, "Be sober, be vigilant; because your adversary the devil walks about like a roaring lion, seeking whom he may devour." The Enemy has not divided his attacks against mankind based on class, race, wealth, or education. Satan seeks anyone who wavers in their commitment to the Father. Also, he will attack anyone in any classification of life to persuade their commitment by employing the spirit of the anti-Christ.

There are many communities globally who are impacted by classism. The American Heritage College dictionary defines classism as a bias based on a person, family, or communities social or economic class. Satan leverage's his initiatives using social and cultural divides. The divides are his attempt to flank (charge from the outside) the Kingdom of God. If Satan can antagonize people by making them afraid of each other, then it lessens the chance for them to experience the love of God. Division initiated by Satan are not just wealth or economic divides. Internal classism will develop when there are people who take on their own agenda to declassify what they believe is right or wrong. This can be a door to discrimination, hatred, and segregation. Thomas Sowell says,

"Words can also be misleading when insinuating a fictitious sameness among things that happen to be called by the same name--- such as "income" that includes both salaries and capital gains, or "education" measured by years of schooling rather than by the amount, kind or quality of learning that takes place. When people with the "same" education receive different incomes, that is often called discrimination..."[12]

In Satan's plan, he uses discrimination to keep 'race wars' alive in the earth. When there is racial tension and conflict, he understands that there will be multiple divides in the church. People will be divided by their feelings, experience, and their perspective on racial pride.

There is nothing wrong with having pride one's human existence until one person or group of people desire supreme dominance over another race. When Satan ignite race wars in the earth, his agenda is to divide the Kingdom of God on multiple levels. In many cases, his goal is to induce levels of hatred that makes reconciliation impossible. Reconciliation cannot happen without forgiveness and understanding being the forerunner of that initiative. Ken Wytsma says, "When we address racism, we often make the mistake of trying to resolve the problem without diagnosing or understanding what or who created it in the first place."[13] Satan knows that is common for people to not listen to each other, therefore this war tactic works well in disrupting the security and safety of people. When this happens, it can cause ethnic groups to question God's role in the racial conflict; in other times it can cause people to place a supremacy on God's responsibility to respond to their race above all others. God's agenda is about building His Kingdom in the earth.

God's Kingdom includes nations, race, ethnicities, and cultures. However, when the enemy begin to lose the battle in 'race wars', he then will turn to wealth and prosperity. He uses money as a way for believers to attribute their success in financial gains. But it must be stated, that all financial gains do not come because a person has practiced Christian principles. Therefore, there are times when people are perplexed about God's provisional hand and His thoughts on poverty. When it comes to wealth, the Enemy complicates mankind's understanding about God's earthly financial plan by contrasting it with the immediate rewards stated his agenda. Psalms 37 vs. 1-11 shares this complication.

[1] Do not fret because of evildoers, Nor be envious of the workers of iniquity.

² For they shall soon be cut down like the grass, And wither as the green herb.

³ Trust in the Lord, and do good; Dwell in the land, and feed on His faithfulness.
⁴ Delight yourself also in the Lord, And He shall give you the desires of our heart.
⁵ Commit your way to the Lord, Trust also in Him, And He shall bring *it* to pass.
⁶ He shall bring forth your righteousness as the light, And your justice as the noonday. ⁷ Rest in the Lord, and wait patiently for Him; Do not fret because of him who prospers in his way, Because of the man who brings wicked schemes to pass.
⁸ Cease from anger, and forsake wrath; Do not fret— *it* only *causes* harm. ⁹ For evildoers shall be cut off; But those who wait on the Lord, They shall inherit the earth. ¹⁰ For yet a little while and the wicked *shall be* no *more;* Indeed, you will look carefully for his place, But it *shall be* no *more.* ¹¹ But the meek shall inherit the earth, And shall delight themselves in the abundance of peace.

Here, the Psalmist identifies that there are "evildoers" and "workers of iniquity." He begins his discourse by stating that you do not need to be worried. In v.9 he reminds that reader that "evildoers" will be cut off, and those who wait on God will "inherit" the earth. This applies to wealth and financial gains because a person does not have to uses the ways of the wicked to walk in the harvest of God. However, the enemy will apply pressure to life just as he did to Job, this can cause a person to agree to things that are not congruent with their faith or discipline moving forward financially. This can be considered the great financial compromise.

Satan uses wealth and the hope of wealth to disable the profession of the believer. It is not God's desire that mankind live as vagabonds or indentured servants. Neither is it the plan of God for His people to be indebted to governments and kingdoms. Satan employs strategies in the earth to keep humans in his matrix. He uses the spirit of bondage to multiple ways. When this spirit is in operation, it does not only keep the poor being poor, but it causes also causes wealthy or successful people. Therefore, people will live outside of their means intentionally to not appear to others as though they are poor.

If family is lives in poverty, that does not mean that they must remain in that situation. In Matthew 26, there was a woman who had an alabaster box of oil. She used the oil to anoint Jesus, as she proceeded to pour the oil, the disciples saw it as a mismanagement of resources. They would have preferred that it be sold and used to care for the poor. When resources are being used, Satan can create internal conflict within the family, organization, or ministry to further induce his plan to divide the community. Satan does not care about the poor being bettered or changed. His strategic plan to induce poverty is two-fold, in which he employs poverty as a nuclear weapon against people. Poverty has an infection radius just like a nuclear weapon explosion and contamination radius. When poverty rules a land, Satan knows that it is easier for him to institute plans that will bring people to damnation. Therefore, the economic status of man is impacted by systematic racism, institutional monopolies, and organized spiritual wickedness.

The Enemy uses different strategies to accomplish many initiatives that are set in his strategic plan. With his goal being the perpetual terrorizing the earth to push his agenda against God's Kingdom. Another strategy that he employs is his fight against education. Satan knows that people will remain desperate and scattered when education is attacked. He uses several methods to work wickedness within education. Education is important in every community. Because the world is governed by the import and export of goods, education is needed to maintain the growth of kingdoms and nations. Satan has systemic institutionalized wickedness that is designed to keep people divided and society bound to his plan.

For some critics, this is a sign of the catastrophic failure of an establishment-led effort to increase education from the top down: Building schools and hiring teachers is useless if there is no strong underlying demand for education; conversely, if there is a real demand for skill, a demand for education will naturally emerge, and supply will follow. --- So, if the failure of schools in developing countries to attract children can't be explained by problems of access, or lack of demand for educated labor, or parent resistance to education their children, then where is the snag?[14]

Education is important in every country. Satan understands intelligence. Therefore, if he can make education less important in the heart of students then he is able to implement plans that carry long-term effects on a nation. There are students that complain about the academic workload, many of whom have the potential to manage the workload without a problem. However, the Enemy uses enticement to persuade the generation to come. 1 Peter 2 vs. 9-10 says, "But you *are* a chosen generation, a royal priesthood, a holy nation, His own special people, that you may proclaim the praises of Him who called you out of darkness into His marvelous light, who once *were* not a people but *are* now the people of God, who had not obtained mercy but now have obtained mercy." Satan fights against the generation to come by changing the images of success. Therefore, he can distract students from dreaming to become contributing citizens in their communities.

Even in education, Satan can deploy agents to ignite racial divide and employ systemic racism, and classism in academic institutions. His objective by doing this will always be to oppress and suppress and generation from rising. The Enemy is so cunning that he can use the grading system to suppress a generation of students in every level. Also, he uses the class system in education dualistically. A student can be judged by their peers based on where they come from and how they perform in school. Students can also be judged by faculty and staff based on class. They can be given access, opportunity and support in ways that are biased and unfair. This type of criticism is essential to the enemy when he is trying to advance his plan in inequality. There will always be an economic divide when there are social classes, social status, social acceptance, and social etiquettes. The Enemy is good at turning these classifications into platforms to initiate racial disharmony. He suppresses the dreams of humans that are not able to persevere beyond their experience(s).

There were two students who attended a school. One was Albert, who was an African American from a rural community. The other was named Josh, who was Caucasian from a middle-class privileged experience. They both were in the same academic program. Over the years, Albert and Josh grew to learn more of each other because there were opportunities granted in school that they both shared in, this produced a mutual respect between the two students. As the students journeyed through the program, they did not see their ethnicity as a problem or hindrance from them being friends. As time progressed, they both reached their end goal, which was graduation. In their final semester they shared their final experience in the same course. At the beginning of the course, nervousness and excited feels every classroom. Albert and Josh began the journey to finish their final course together and further life. During the course, the students would have open discussion about their reading that was facilitated by the instructor. There was one day when Albert got the shock of his life. On this day, Josh was responding and mentioned aloud that this was the "first book" that he read since being at the institution.

Albert and other brown and black people were astonished by this announcement. There were many questions and emotions that bombarded Albert at one-time. Unfortunately, he was only able to share he feelings with his minority peers that shared some of the same feelings. As hard as Albert worked to matriculate through the program, it was appalling to hear from a fellow student that they reached graduation by not having to put in half of the effort to reach the end. There are many instances around the world where Satan plants these types of situations. We are not saying that Josh was employed by Satan, but we are saying that any academic system that creates advantages for students with backgrounds of privilege, wealth, parents who are government leaders, public figures can be used by Satan to keep people oppressed.

Both Albert and Josh were on their own paths to discovering what was next for their life. However, any institution that does not uphold the standard for performance from all students buys into Satan's systemic racism and social class division plan. Evil is not an action of a race or color of people; evil is hidden in the intent of the heart. Satan employs evil in the earth. Just as important as it is to know Satan's plan, it is just as important to know his identity, character, attributes, and manifestation.

2
Satan's ID

⁴Yea, though I walk through the valley of the shadow of death,
I will fear no evil;
For You *are* with me;
Your rod and Your staff, they comfort me.

⁵You prepare a table before me in the presence of my enemies;
You anoint my head with oil;
My cup runs over.

                                            Psalm 23

When the name Satan is mentioned, immediately he is recognized as the "Devil" in a lot of Christian and non-Christian communities. From Genesis to Revelation, Satan is seen as a being who terrorizes the earth in the context of the bible. Unfortunately, if the "Devil's" identification is not properly accessed throughout Christian history, then, Christians today could find themselves challenged in being able to identify the "Devil" in context in this modern day. Throughout Christian history, Satan's identity has evolved. He has been given different names, but he remains the same character.

Satan having different names would be like your parents and friends creating a nickname for you. Nicknames are other names that are used to acknowledge or address you, however, nicknames do not replace the name given at birth. Overtime Satan was giving different names that are used intime to identify him. Some of those names are Devil, Enemy, Lucifer, Snake and the Father of Lies. It is not wrong to use any of these names in addressing the Devil, however, it is necessary to understand the evolution of the use of these names. Paul uses the name Satan repetitively throughout Corinthians and Romans. In 2 Corinthians 2 vs. 11 Paul says, "Lest Satan should take advantage of us; for we are not ignorant of his devices." However, before understanding this passage in the context in which Paul is using the name Satan, it is necessary to examine the history of his name and its use.

In Genesis chapter 3, a new character is introduced in the creation story. The new character is the "serpent." In some Christian communities, when this story is read, it is assumed that the serpent is Satan in this text. In this text, there are attributes that will remain consistent with the attributes of the Enemy. In verse 1 of Genesis chapter, the writer describes the serpent as the most cunning beast of the field. This story carries the introduction of the concept of evil more so than the introduction of Satan as a being or figure. Tony W. Cartledge says,

"The concept of Satan as the source of evil and chief of demons developed rather late in the Old Testament period, probably based on ideas picked up from the Persians, following the exile. Prior to the development of this more dualistic view, and apart from an understanding of evil as an abstract quality inherent in humankind, evil, like everything else, was thought to come from God."[1]

It is important to acknowledge the entrance of evil. As we engage in spiritual battles, the Enemy can be addressed by his aliases but, if we fail to recognize his attributes knowing his name only is fruitless. Satan does not play fair, neither does he use rules of engagement in war that are ethical. He has made it his duty to be disruptive and luring. The spirit of seduction is not employed by the Enemy to draw mankind into promiscuity or infidelity only, his duty is to ultimately draw mankind's love away from God. James 1 vs. 14-15 says, "But each one is tempted when he is drawn away by his own desires and enticed. Then, when desire has conceived, it gives birth to sin; and sin, when it is full-grown, brings forth death." In the book of James, he mentions how the devil tempts us with evil. He shares how God does not tempt His children but because of the evil nature of Satan, he will manipulate mankind's desire to execute evil intention and ways in the heart of man.

Zoroaster

He was an east Iranian prophet who followers worshipped the deity Ahura-Mazda. They believed in divine beings and was associated with older Aryan religion. Zoroaster believed that the world was divided into three ages of three thousand year intervals. He classified this ages as: the first was the golden age of Ahura-Mazda, the second was a period of warfare with evil that ended with the coming of Zoroaster, the third would be the renovation of the world.

Therefore, in Genesis 3, the serpent in Hebrew means שָׁחָשׁ **nâchâsh**, a snake (from its hiss).[2] The serpent was the beast that introduced evil to mankind. Over time the development of Satan being a deity was introduced by Zoroaster teaching. However, as we engage in spiritual battles, it is necessary to note that the enemy will employ skills that he has attained through time to trick the individuals into supporting his agenda unconsciously.

The story of man's fall is not the only story in the bible that display the development of Satan's character. Therefore it is important for us to understand what happens with Satan throughout scripture. Satan is deceptive. It is his desire that he would be able to trick mankind being familiar with his name and ignorant of his devices.

2 Corinthians v. 11 says, "lest Satan should take advantage of

us; for we are not ignorant of his devices." First and foremost, because we have been redeemed out of the hands of the enemy, every believer should have a basic working knowledge of Satan. This working knowledge should give the believer intelligence about the Enemy and his tactics. However, it is easy to overlook demonic influence that come in good deeds, great messages or in the form of help. Because one of the attributes of the enemy is to deceive, he can offer great things or opportunities that are a camouflage for his true motive.

When Jesus was sent to be tempted of the Devil in the wilderness, Satan presented Him with three offers. The first offer was an interrogation of His power. Satan wanted Jesus to use is power to turn stone into bread. The second offer was for Jesus to throw Himself down into the holy city. Satan challenged Jesus with the word of God, taunting him by quoting Scripture, "For it is written: 'He shall give His angels charge over you,' and, 'In their hands they shall bear you up, lest you dash your foot against a stone.'" The third offer, Satan tried to bribe Jesus by showing Him the kingdoms of the world and their glory. It is correct to know that Satan is cunning, but Satan uses more than a cunning nature to implement his deceit and manipulation. In his interaction with Jesus, we can see three things in effect. He employs the tactics of persuasion, giving incentives, and falsification as a hoax against Jesus. Satan desires for mankind to know his name but remain ignorant of his ways.

Demonology is an area in the kingdom of God that is ridiculed, manipulated, and received with skepticism. Entertainment has distorted our perspective of gods, demonic activity, and spiritual possession. Society has adopted a skeptic view of our interaction with the dark world. Sometimes the church walks in fear of gods, demons, and spirits because we lack tangible knowledge of recognizing them and their effect in human lives. It is challenging for a person to identify negative influences in their life if demonic activity is submerged in their culture. When we are consumed by our culture or communities, it is possible to not be able to recognize ill behaviors, thoughts, or behavior patterns that are demonically influenced. Satan does not desire for believers to show forth productivity and/or peace of mind. Therefore, he torments the earth with his agenda. He uses demonic devices to employ his vices upon people, families, communities, and regions.

One of the devices that Satan uses upon mankind is scarcity. When scarcity is present, Satan uses it as an opportunity to employ tactics like persuasion and incentives in moments of scarcity. Remember in Matthew 4 vs. 2, the writer says Jesus fasted forty days and forty nights, and after fasting, Jesus was hungry. Satan immediately engages Jesus and employs these to two tactics persuasion and incentive. William T. Cavanaugh says, "Resources are scarce wherever the desires of all persons for goods and services cannot be met. In other words, hunger is written into the conditions under which economics operates."[4] When things are scarce, Satan can challenge people's truth about God. Scarcity ignites fear about sustainability and survival.

It contradicts God's ability to supply needs and provide, therefore, scarcity presents a theological conflict for many faith believers in Christianity. Imagine the psyche of the Israelites in Egyptian captivity for four hundred years. During this time, they went from famine to captivity. The lack of resources can influence people to make hasty decisions out of desperation about the need to survive. The enemy uses this to cause believers to think more about their ability than God's ability to provide. When economics are challenged, it is easy common to consider the skill of a person or the lack of self-drive that an individual can have as the issue for their lack of success. The enemy understands manipulating humans is different from persuading Angels.

Satan uses manipulative devices against mankind as he employs hidden vices within the culture. He does not care about society remaining civil. His agenda is to keep communities disruptive, uncivil, and in disagreement. By using vices, he can deceive mankind into practicing self-idolatry or demonstrating narcissistic behavior. A vice is an evil, degrading, or immoral practice or habit. In Romans chapter 7, Paul details the war within himself that challenged his moral compass in being good. Verse 21 says, "I find then a law, that evil is present with me, the one who wills to do good." Satan uses the source of evil to disrupt our harmony with God. Dr. Darlene Powell Hopson and Dr. Derek S. Hopson says, "specifically concerning soul, we believe that if you have an open, strong connection to soul, you project the positive energy that the connection produces."[5] The enemy knows that good should come out of the soul. Therefore, he employs things that can awaken the desire of mankind in efforts of darkening the good of the soul by blemished character.

The *Seven Capital vices* recognized in modern theology is traditionally known as *the seven deadly sins.* These strongholds of the soul have been the bedrock of theological conversation before the inception of the church. Man has always struggled with the fight between *his will* and God's *perfect will.* James 1 vs. 14 says, "But each one is tempted when he is drawn away by his own desires and enticed."

Satan knows that mankind has two detrimental weaknesses, which are curiosity and desire. Rebecca DeYoung says, "a study of personal vices can be a catalyst for spiritual growth."[6]

The seven capital vices are: envy, vainglory, sloth, avarice, anger, gluttony, and lust. The forefathers considered these to be elements within human nature that become the foundation for all sinful nature of man. Therefore, Rebecca DeYoung suggests that if we are clueless to these sins and their application in our modern time, then we can become negligent of caring for our soul. These vices were often contrasted with the virtues that Christians should possess. It was believed that the vices were and enemy of a virtuous life. "The seven capital vices are the set of vices that grow out of pride and tend to proliferate additional sin."[7]

Satan creates war against God's chosen. The reason for the fight is to challenge the progression of the confession of Christ in the earth. Matthew 11 vs 12 says, "[12] And from the days of John the Baptist until now the kingdom of heaven suffers violence, and the violent take it by force." This verse is commonly interpreted in many communities to imply for a person to remain strong in Christ, they must fight harder than the enemy. A more appropriate response to that verse is to understand that the Kingdom of God has been under siege since the inception, and every attack against this kingdom is carried out violently. Therefore, Satan uses things like vices because they are easy to go undetected and misinterpreted in modern day Christian communities. Moreover, these vices are potent and deadly when they have been employed.

Let's look at envy, it is a feeling of discontent and resentment aroused by desire. Mark 7 vs. 21-23 says,

> "[21] For from within, out of the heart of men, proceed evil thoughts, adulteries, fornications, murders, [22] Thefts, covetousness, wickedness, deceit, lasciviousness, an evil eye, blasphemy, pride, foolishness: [23] All these evil things come from within, and defile the man."

ENVY

Envy does not manifest be its definition, moreover it is accompanied by its family member's jealousy, covetousness, and greed. Life is not about competing against each other or desiring what others have, however, the enemy uses the tool of marketing to push people's desire to the edge. Every enticing thing does not come because of direct jealousy of someone that is known, but we must include the indirect notions that men harbor because of what has been shown to them. DeYoung believes that covetousness and greed are possession driven. These would be the elements that would push a person to live outside of their financial means because of being driven to live out their desires now. The best lives lived, are those who live their lives with a plan, discipline, and strategy for success.

"Envy, on the other hand, is typically more concerned with who we are. Envy targets internal qualities of another person, qualities that give a person worth, honor, standing, or status."[8] Satan uses this vice to cause people to ignore the greatness within them. Not only does he want them to ignore it, but he does not want them to determine within themselves to develop or process the greatness within them. Envy can have a person adopting mentors and coaches relentlessly because of their attraction to the inner beauty of someone else. When envy is employed and active, the individual denies themselves of predestination. Like when God spoke to Jeremiah about being ordained before being formed within his mother, it is evident that God has a predestined plan for each person.

The enemy is never afraid of a person's potential; the enemy is afraid of a person determination to transform potential into intentional positive outcomes. Therefore, the vice of envy can have a person chase every possession or status that they can obtain in efforts of displaying success. However, materialistic possession does not allow display the wellness of the soul. Envy will cause a person to overlook their wellness by modeling others intensely. This does not mean that you will not have down days or seasons of disappointment; this means, when you become envious, you become a playground for the enemy to unsettle your emotions, plans, and commitments. He uses this because envy will become an immediate opposing force to one's progress in God.

VAINGLORY

Vainglory is boastful, unwarranted pride in one's accomplishments or qualities. There is a difference in vainglory and having self-confidence. Everyone must believe in themselves to walk in progress and achievement. However, Satan uses vainglory to drive attention and recognition. In the modern time, the enemy has used the worldwide web as a platform to employ vainglory in the lives of people. People seek recognition and acknowledgement at an alarming rate because of internet accessibility. The enemy uses that to his advantage to destroy relationships, break-up homes, and demolish working systems. Psalm 51 vs 10-11 says,

"¹⁰ Create in me a clean heart, O God; and renew a right spirit within me. ¹¹ Cast me not away from thy presence; and take not thy holy spirit from me." Vainglory is deceptive against our Christian walk.

It is important to know that God remains a jealous God. When the Psalmist is asking for God to clean their heart and not cast them out of His presence, it is a critical statement. This is important because we see in scripture that God's presence cannot be destroyed, but He can decide to move His glory. Vainglory is a vice that can cause us to become absent of God's presence. Rebecca DeYoung says, "when caught in the vice of vainglory, we want acclaim too much, so much, in fact, that we will accept it where it is deserved or not."[9] Satan knows that God is a jealous God. He knows of God's ability to remove His glory and dismiss people out of His presence. Satan understands when people embrace vainglory that they will manage their commitment to God based on who acknowledges or recognizes their commitment in God.

This becomes a crippling agent in Christian context; simply because this vice will attach itself to other vices with the intent to dismantle good works and destroy good people. The enemy makes vainglory undetectable because he blends it with pride. However, vainglory and pride are two different things. "The spirit of haughtiness (pride) would like to keep us from becoming the creation God wants to make of us---namely, the best people we can possible be."[10] Satan understands the complication with pride in the relationship to God. When vainglory and pride are present, it can cause the believer to ignore redirection, transformation, and self-awareness.

The weapon of vainglory is weapon commonly used in Satan's ploy to stop the kingdom of God from advancing. When he employs these tactics, he can dissolve the perspective of Christ's love in the earth. He will engage these vices by using scriptural discrepancies and God-like principles to persuade the believer away from God. Pride is an excessive concern with excelling over others; vainglory, by contrast, concerns primarily the display or manifestation of excellence[11]. Satan does not care if we miss the promise of God, but it hurts God heart if we chose to forsake His glory for vainglory. God does not forsake or overlook the faithfulness of His sons and daughters.

SLOTH

Sloth is the aversion of work, or exertion; it is extreme version of laziness. This is another vice that is designed to assassinate the destiny of mankind by opposing diligence. The enemy knows that the implementation of sloth offsets the demonstration of fortitude. Fortitude is one of the four cardinal virtues. It is important to Satan that we know the name of God but do not stand in confidence of that name. Jospef Pieper says, "Fortitude that does not reach down into the depths of willingness to die is spoiled at its roots and devoid of effective power."[12] It is impossible for a person to demonstrate fortitude if they have been cemented by laziness.

Satan is not the father of time. He manipulates time and cause people to ignore their seasons based on the time that has been given to live out their purpose of life. When he employs this weapon, it is common for the devil to disrupt the life of a person and cause them to become overwhelmed by the circumstances of life. When we are overwhelmed by life and its issues, our response to overcoming weakens. The human will have the ability to overcome e challenges and failure, but when you are hopeless, it is difficult to override the feelings and emotions that accompany sloth. "Spiritual battles take place on many fronts. Sometimes bodily pleasures or bodily weariness do make us more susceptible to sin. But in the case of this vice, the battle is first and foremost waged within our hearts."[13]

Satan uses this vice to separate and divide people. It can cause you to be intentional about avoiding people and events. There is more to sloth than a person being lazy. Sloth will cause one to abort their destiny willingly. The devil understands that the Kingdom of God is about productivity and advancement. Therefore, nothing will advance if people are on the wrong side of their commitment. The bible talks about the attributes of Satan being that of killing, stealing, and destroying. Sloth is a destroyer that can go undetected without performing honest assessments of who yourself.

AVARICE

This vice is sometimes not acknowledged but remains a lethal weapon of choice of the enemy. Avarice can be provoked by other vices to entice a person into embracing the war waged within themselves. When this vice is applied, it is more than someone having the nature of greed, it deals with their heart of generosity. People who operate with avarice are challenged in giving on two levels: under-giving and over-giving. The enemy uses this as his weapon of choice to distort the purpose of giving and compassion within Christianity.

Jesus prescribes loving your neighbor as if they were ourselves as the greatest commandment. Satan knows that loving people is a sign of a believer's commitment. Therefore, when a person is battling avarice, they are wrestling with the war waged within their heart. "Greed's inner clutch on the heart can corrode the virtue of generosity and dampen our enthusiasm and eagerness to give freely. At its worst, however, greed also incites us to the obstinate refusal to meet even the demands of basic justice, as we opt instead to keep more than our share."[14] Satan benefits when societies suffer from the lack of advocacy. The manifestation of greed will birth selfishness and/or a self-centered attitude. Therefore, when the devil institutes this vice in people, he knows that it will defy the commandment, "Love thy neighbor as thyself."

ANGER

Ephesians 4 vs 26 says, "[26] Be ye angry, and sin not: let not the sun go down upon your wrath:" Anger is not misunderstood; however, it can be misplaced. This word can appear as a contradiction of love. Especially in communication, anger can appear as though someone has temporary loss love for the thing that they are angry about. Satan uses anger to blemish the character of people by implementing it as a tool to force disharmony and separation amongst people. He distorts the function of anger in the hearts of people.

Anger should not be used as a weapon between two individuals. Rather, anger can be used speak up for people, and is a critical element in advocacy. It is a critical element that connects to passion and justice. Justice can only be instituted when anger has been voiced. "Anger must serve the cause, not the other way around. Venting the emotion is not itself the point; in fact, expressing anger to let off steam is often a moral mistake."[14] When anger is pointed towards one another, the enemy builds strife within the community.

Division is not a point of disagreeing on terms or decisions. A community divides when it becomes angry at each other for the terms or decisions that have been made. The source of anger that presents itself can cause people to opt out of listening, reasoning, and rationalizing for understanding. Misappropriation of anger has led to bad leaders in society. Various communities have suffered from murder, dictatorships, genocide, slavery, etc. These behaviors were the manifestation of anger that is unjust. Therefore, the enemy uses anger in efforts of trying to discredit a just God and a righteous kingdom.

GLUTTONY

Gluttony is defined two ways: A person who eats or consumers immoderately and a person with an inordinate capacity to receive or withstand something. Satan employs gluttony by intertwining it with other vices. "As a vice, gluttony is something habitual. It is a routine, a pattern, or a groove that gets worn into our character."[15] Satan prefers that mankind focus on gluttony in relationship to food only. But when we look at the depth of gluttony, it is activated by lust and held in place by other vices simultaneously. This weapon is vicious because it can cause people to live beyond their means.

We can overextend ourselves with gluttony. This vice has an emotional and psychological expense. When gluttony is not detected by a person, they pay the price daily. "Most people living with less than 99 cents a day do not seem to act as if they are starving. If they were, surely, they would put every available penny into buying more calories. But they do not. ---The poor seem to have many choices, and they don't elect to spend as much as they can on food."[16] Gluttony survives on the need to have and the lack of discipline. In the story of Jesus being taken into the wilderness to be tempted of the devil, Satan tempted Jesus to turn stones into bread, it is these moments of need that people must watch the awakening of desire.

Satan seeks whom he may devour. Gluttony is readily used as a way of destroying your economic stability. Gluttony destroys the economy when the need to have more things and stuff have become a sense of accomplishment or gratification. When countries spike taxes, and the cost of living inflates for a family of four who's income hasn't changed, an economic restraint is bound to happen. For example, there is a family of four who looks for food daily, however, to function today, the need to survive goes beyond food.

LUST

Lust is the vice that challenges a person's sexual appetite against their desire for companionship. The is Satan's weapon of choice. He uses this vice in many areas of life. It is designed to keep people challenged and in disharmony with God and each other. Sexual fulfillment without marriage provides temporary gratification. When this vice is active, it can permit a person to fulfill their sexual desire at the expense of losing part of themselves. It is the will of Satan to have mankind live without restraint or self-control.

Rebecca DeYoung says, "Lust is a vice, then because it does not honor the fullness of sex, and it alienates people from each other just when they are supposed to be experiencing intimate union. There's a betrayal of meaning in lust's use of sex for nothing but self-gratification, and it is difficult to be lustful without feeling that loss at some level."[16] Lust is something that causes a person to become selfish. It can have a person willing to fulfill their own desires at any cost.

The expense of lust will lead to a loss of trust in any relationship. Good people can become deeply wounded by the actions of this vice. The enemy understands that this vice can cause a person to become a prisoner to their own desire. Ultimately, Satan desires that mankind die at the cost of their own sin. James 1 vs 15, "Then when lust hath conceived, it bringeth forth sin: and sin, when it is finished, bringeth forth death." Satan uses lust to darken mankind's understanding of God's grace.

The aftereffects of lustful fulfillment can cause a person to feel condemned and not fit to be used by God. Condemnation is not permissible for the believer to place on themselves; therefore, the enemy will allow the person to discredit themselves and choose not to be used because of their guilt. In addition to not being used by God, lust can breach trust, burden relationships and break-up friendships. Satan knows this vice can have a person think inwardly about their needs without considering how the other person will feel or interpret the action. Lust operates like a grenade; it can destroy anything within its radius in a matter of seconds.

When scripture invites us to not be ignorant to the devil's devices, it is important to know the basics about his vices. He does not have a vested interest in the welfare of mankind or society. The earth is Satan's domain: he is not looking to build the earth or advance God's plan. His agenda is to build and enlarge his kingdom by the ignorance of man's understanding. In order to continue perpetuating his rebellion, he desires for mankind to forsake the covenant that God made with Himself and man.

3
Devil Strategic Plan

¹Make a joyful shout to the LORD, all you lands!
² Serve the LORD with gladness;
Come before His presence with singing.³ Know that the LORD, He *is* God;
It is He *who* has made us, and not we ourselves;
We are His people and the sheep of His pasture

Psalm 100

Satan has an agenda for his kingdom and a strategic plan for mankind. 1 Peter 5 vs 8 says, "Be sober, be vigilant; because your adversary the devil, as a roaring lion, walketh about, seeking whom he may devour:". The adversary's agenda is to prohibit the grace of God to be demonstrated in the earth for mankind. It would be easy to say that the enemy desires to "kill the church." Satan has been an opposing force against the birth of the church upon conception. In the New Testament, King Herod released a decree to kill all of the first-born male children during Jesus's time. For over two thousand years the church continues to experience resistance and opposition. Satan uses a variety of tactics to seek for people in hopes of devouring them.

He does not just only attack individuals, but Satan can attack families, cities, regions, and territories. Satan will do whatever is relevant with the present times to confuse people about the grace of God. His agenda includes him releasing the spirit of the antichrist in the earth. "The spirit of antichrist is actively shaping world opinion to accept the devil's counterfeit for Christ."[1] Satan opposes men and women being exposed to the knowledge of Christ. Moreover, he does not want mankind to experience Christ's love and power. Therefore, he strategically uses poverty, unforgiveness, education, gender, and theology against society.

Satan knows that believers can be dressed in the armor of God which will thwart his attacks. When believers are dressed in the armor, they are not susceptible to responding to his games and plans outside of God's leading. In Ephesians 6, Paul describes the armor and its necessity.

> "[10] Finally, my brethren, be strong in the Lord, and in the power of his might. [11] Put on the whole armour of God, that ye may be able to stand against the wiles of the devil. [12] For we wrestle not against flesh and blood, but against principalities, against powers, against the rulers of the darkness of this world, against spiritual wickedness in high places.

> ¹³ Wherefore take unto you the whole armour of God, that ye may be able to withstand in the evil day, and having done all, to stand. ¹⁴ Stand therefore, having your loins girt about with truth, and having on the breastplate of righteousness; ¹⁵ And your feet shod with the preparation of the gospel of peace; ¹⁶ Above all, taking the shield of faith, wherewith ye shall be able to quench all the fiery darts of the wicked. ¹⁷ And take the helmet of salvation, and the sword of the Spirit, which is the word of God:"

Ephesians 6: 10-17 KJV

Having the armor of God enables the believer to stand beyond their natural ability to stand in trying times. When a believer is dressed, the understand that the ultimate war is waged in the spirit realm or cosmos. Derek Prince says, "I believe that Satan particularly fears the ministry of deliverance for two reasons: First, because, again, it brings his invisible kingdom out into the open. --- Second, because it shows the supremacy and victory of God's kingdom over Satan's kingdom."² When the armor of God is present, it demonstrates to the enemy that the person is ready for battle.

The armor includes: the helmet of salvation, sword of the Spirit, shield of faith, loins girded with truth, feet covered with peace, and the breastplate of righteousness. This spiritual body armor is necessary in producing the four cardinal virtues: prudence, justice, fortitude, and temperance. The devil opposes people because it is a sign of God's grace, and it is evidence of God being present in the earth. The devil's tactics are designed to disarm believers' faith and disengage their belief in God's promises and ability.

In cases of economic dilapidation and social destruction, it is hard for mankind to reason God's faithfulness in times of despair. In the year of 2020, *the world health organization* declared COVID-19 as a pandemic. This pandemic did not only effect people, but it shook the church greatly. Because of the number of rapid and unexpected deaths, people of the church did not know whether God was cleaning up the church because of sin or if the untimely deaths were happening because of a modern-day plague. Satan will use anything he can to leverage his deceptive ways to cause people to contradict their belief in Christ. This is not a new strategy that the enemy has invited for the modern world.

In various times in bible history there are instances where the devil employed the same tactics to discourage and confuse a nation. When the children were leaving Egypt, they began to communicate their fear because of the threat and presence of their enemy. The moment they began to communicate their fear, they were willing to reenter captivity because they lacked assurance in God about His ability to deliver them from their enemy. Frank and Ida Mae Hammond say's,

> "The battle is very personal and close. --- The weapons are spiritual. --- This tells us that Satan's tactic is to put pressure on us. He does this in the areas of our thought life, emotions, decision making, and our physical bodies. --- When one is ignorant of Satan's devices he may turn for relief to tranquilizers, sleeping pills, or even the psychiatrist's couch. But God's remedy for victory over demonic pressures is spiritual warfare."[3]

Spiritual warfare is being taught all over the world. However, learning spiritual warfare should not make us more conscious of the devil and become negligent of God's ability and power.

The Devil is elusive and intentional about the implementation of his plans and schemes. He manipulates people with a distorted truth of the word of God. He will cause scripture to become heretical. His intent is to make a hybrid Christianity. A type of religion that honors the name of God but denies the power and resurrection of His son. Hybrid Christianity will create mutant believers. In 2 Timothy 3 vs 4-7 says,

> "[4] Traitors, heady, highminded, lovers of pleasures more than lovers of God;[5] Having a form of godliness, but denying the power thereof: from such turn away. [6] For of this sort are they which creep into houses, and lead captive silly women laden with sins, led away with divers lusts, [7] Ever learning, and never able to come to the knowledge of the truth."

Mutant believers will be people who use religion only as a factor in their life but not willing to commit to any form of personal transformation. The Devil prefers for mankind to have a type of Christianity without possessing a true conviction in Jesus Christ.

Therefore, the enemy uses offense and unforgiveness in spiritual battles like a gas or substance is used in chemical warfare. The enemy knows the potency of unforgiveness. Unforgiveness can affect every area of a person's life. It can walk with a person for many years. This weapon cannot be used without offense being present. Shirley Vinson says, "The devil knows that we will never be able to avoid offenses, they are going to come. However, the devil wants us to hold offenses in our hearts because it gives him access to our mind; thereby he has access to our ability to reason."[4] Everyone knows that they let offense go, however, depending on the type of offense will determine the type of assistance needed to walkout forgiveness.

This strategy of offense and unforgiveness when employed by the enemy can separate you from God. Because God is love and practices forgiveness, the innate ability to love and forgive lives within us when we become a child of the King. Strategically Satan uses these weapons to disrupt relationships and annihilate working relationships within societies. Disruptions can take place in families, communities, and people. In the book of Amos chapter three, Amos asks the question about two people walking together in agreement. Agreement is a Christ-like attribute in the kingdom of God. Consequently, the devil does not like agreement with God. "Forgiveness means we renounce vengeance and retaliation, but it does not mean passive acquiescence to abuse."[5] Practicing forgiveness does not mean a person should become passive or oblivious to a person's hatred towards them.

The enemy's plan is to make the Kingdom of God appear fictitious and unreal in the earth. It is difficult for people who have experienced hatred or racism to fathom God's grace on earth, especially when there is racism, extreme radicals, dictators, and genocide. In this world, the devil desire for people to be afraid and live tormented by fear. When human life is not valued, Satan exercises fear in the heart of mankind, this gives him the opportunity to employ slavery in our present day.

Slavery

1.   The state of one bound in servitude as the property of a slaveholder or household. 2a. The practice of owning slaves. b. A mode of production in which slaves constitute the principal work force. 3. The condition of being subject or addicted to a specified influence. 4. A condition of hard work and subjection.

Slavery in the modern is not displayed in its traditional form. In former days, it was common to see people traded and purchased to build a family or tribal nation's legacy. Today, slavery is not as blatant or obvious as in the past; he has constructed a modern slave plan that continues to devalue human life. In modern times, Satan uses taxes, inflation, education inequality, classism, entertainment, athletics, and religious segregation to institute slavery. These things combined will continue to create a wealth gap. The benefit of Satan modernizing slavery with each generation increases the wealth gap means the poverty line will increase; therefore, causing more people to become challenged with daily survival.

As destruction increases in the earth, Satan uses that as an opportunity to distort the truth about God's unmeasurable ability. Every opposing force against the kingdom of God knows that God's ability is not limited or capped. The only way that he can be limited is if He is limited in the mind of people.

One way that Satan is forcing his agenda in the earth, is through education inequality. He is creating a divide that could possibly reinstitute dictatorships or ownership of people in the earth. My personal observation of education inequality around the world has been alarming. Unless students attend a private institution, the liberty to receive education is open around the world. However, the quality of education is not the same for all people. The quality of jobs that enter a region are based on the average education of residents in the area where the company will plant its business. What becomes problematic is the cost of living. It is not uncommon for paygrades to be established based on the economy of the region and the education of the individual.

The reason Satan would drive the concept of education inequality is because it will fuel the concern of all other injustices that are commonly addressed, such as, race, money, sexuality, and human rights. In third world countries, the education in rural communities is not as in-depth as education in the city. In America, public education is being challenged in many communities while private education is on the rise in cost. Families are making decisions to try to provide opportunities for their children to advance in this competitive world. When people do not know the power of education, they will minimize their opportunities and abilities. This is a critical notion because if a person does not know what they can achieve through basic education, they will potentially settle to live oppressed lifestyles, or reside in oppressed regions hopeless and negligent of their purpose.

A biblical example of this concept in effect is found in Genesis 41 through Exodus 1. In Genesis 41, Pharaoh had a dream that was interpreted by Joseph. In the dream, it was mentioned that there would be a famine in the land. A famine is a drastic wide-reaching food shortage. Joseph was manager of the distribution of goods. During this time, his brothers were sent to Egypt to find food by the instructions of their father. There was corn in Egypt. When economies are struggling, people will move based on desperation and their need to survive without considering God's direction or leading. There are many instances in scripture where people made decisions out of desperation and not being led or visited by God. That is the desire of the Satan, he desires that mankind live their lives based on intuition and not being led by God.

When the Hebrews were in Egypt there was an administration change in Exodus. The bible says that the incoming Pharaoh did not know Joseph, therefore, the favor they incurred was stripped away. However, this passage of scripture demonstrates oppression and economic stress upon people, and how they behave. The new Pharaoh knew that the Hebrews were smart and strong. However, because of being oppressed the Hebrews did not know that about themselves, as a result, they remained under Egyptian oppression for four hundred years. Satan uses these types of strategies upon nations to keep people lacking trust in God the father. It is Satan's desire for people to discredit God and his ability.

Even when nations experience mass killings and/or genocide, the Devil does not want to take the blame for his involvement in such behaviors. He spends his time attacking the character of God. It is his strategy to use character assassination as a weapon in efforts to get more people to consult their intuition in the midst of crisis, instead of consulting God. Matthew 6 vs 33 says, "But seek ye first the kingdom of God, and his righteousness; and all these things shall be added unto you."

Satan's agenda includes using natural disasters and unexpected ordeals to persuade people into not believing in God. He does not care if the disbelief is intentional or subliminal; neither does he want mankind to put their trust in the risen savior. Every time someone puts their trust in the savior, it defies the works of the enemy.

His agenda remains the same, but his strategic plan is complex. He will use lies, gossip, frustrations, and all to cause believers to lose hope in Christ. In the dark world, Satan is not looking to destroy the earth because his ultimate plan is to torment human beings and deter them from believing in the resurrection of Christ. As the prince of darkness, he incorporates denials, family disruptions, financial challenges into his mix of tricks, hoping to frustrate people.

Satan's attributes of seeking, killing, and destroying are true. He purposes in his plan to discredit the work of Christ and stop the advancement of the church. When Christ gave Peter the keys to the kingdom in Matthew 16, He also told Peter that the gates of Hell will not prevail against the church. This was an indication that the opposing force would initiate efforts to stop the progression of the church. Therefore, Satan tries to benefit from social and economic discrepancies in the earth. He begins to use his authority to release order to his angels.

IDENTIFYING THE ENEMY'S PLAN

There are times, when identifying the enemy's plan can be challenge. The devil specializes in camouflaging his motives, plans, and attacks. He has the capability to use anyone unaware by confusing communication, manipulating situations, altering a person's perception, and deceiving people through the word of God. There have been dictators who thought they were doing God's work by ordering mass killings of human beings. During the time of slavery, there were many plantation owners who felt they were doing the work of the Lord by purchasing, trading, and enslaving humans.

Anyplace where there is human oppression by other humans the devil is active. It is not the will or purpose of God for us to oppress each other. The enemy will always desire for people to fight each other. When people are fighting each other, the enemy can insert other tactics and schemes to intensify confusion in societies. Detecting him in social and economic issues is best applied by searching for disharmony between people. There will always be diversity among mankind, however, diversity should not develop into isolation or racism. The devil desires for mankind to destroy its confidence in each other by keeping confusion active in communities, family, and people. When you detect that the enemy is involved in the destruction of relationships or progress, this is the time to apply love towards people. Standing against the enemy when he is terrorizing society requires endurance and awareness. Endurance helps in the longevity of the fight, being aware helps to not be in denial.

Education has been a common battleground for the enemy. The devil attacks academic systems and institutions. Hosea 4 vs 6 says, "My people are destroyed for lack of knowledge: because thou hast rejected knowledge, I will also reject thee, that thou shalt be no priest to me: seeing thou hast forgotten the law of thy God, I will also forget thy children." Satan understands, one way to keep people oppressed is by restricting access to education. Controlling the access is not the only way that he restricts education, but he uses redistricting, teacher retention, academic policies, and legislations to manipulate the accessible for education for people. Basic education should be available to everyone; quality education should be the desired outcome for each institution. However, the enemy will create chaos in the lives of families and students so that he can hide his agenda to oppress people. Chaos effects the student as well as the professional. Detecting the enemy's involvement in education can be seen when people are being segregated by class, ethnicity, and/or demographic. When this is detected, the way to move forward in the battle is by becoming an advocate for change and advancement in education.

Being an advocate may require you to attend school board meetings, meeting with the minister of education, getting with your congressman or member of parliament to address the dilapidation in education. As a believer, the enemy does not expect many believers to possess the courage to standup for those who are voiceless. He uses persecution, consequences, and threats as a way to frighten believers against standing up for those who need a voice. He dares the earth to birth a voice like Moses in the modern day. There have been many voices throughout time that were leaders of change in society. However, the enemy used opposition to serve many voices of change premature deaths. Every country has had someone that was a voice of hope in their society. The enemy will always fight against hope, promise, and progress.

Commonly, people think that the enemy's desire is to increase the wealth gap in society. However, the enemy is more elusive and desires to challenge survival more so than wealth. Satan uses inflation, trade and import and export taxes against the survival of mankind. He does not want anyone people to live in the provision and increase of God. He desires that mankind struggle with sustainability. The devil knows that God is a provider, therefore, he strategically fights against the provision of God. It is not his purpose to help the believer practice good stewardship. It is his goal for believers to live dysfunctional lives and struggle to survive.

The enemy can use money to control the heart of a person. Regardless of a person's financial success, good stewardship remains an ethical and biblical practice of every believer. Satan will attack your finances intentionally. He equates financial challenge to a person becoming willing to question the provisional ability of God. God is not lacking anything, however, when a person is fighting to survive, they can become more susceptible to questioning the existence of God in their life. The story of Job serves as a template for examining the enemy's intention and mankind's response to financial challenges.

In this story, Job was prosperous, yet here was a time when Job experienced affliction in his health, finance, and family, which caused him to be criticized by others. However, Job ultimately displays a resilience in his trust to God that can be demonstrated today. In Job 13 vs 15 he says, "Though he slay me, yet will I trust in him." The enemy becomes frustrated when people display this kind of trust in God.

In addition to identifying education inequality, it is important to identify wealth inequality. Wealth inequality goes beyond the financial challenge of in individual. It is an economic oppression that effects the existence of a group of people and/or nation. Thomas Shapiro says, "Racial inequality appears intransigent because the way families use wealth transmits advantages from generation to generation. --- I see no means of seriously moving toward racial equality without positive asset policies to address the wealth gap."[6]

Financial inequality is demonstrated in various communities through racism, classism, and/or tribalism. Satan uses groupings and classifications to disengage nations trust in God. His is strategic plan is to cause people to believe in God without having faith or baptism in God. Therefore, using financial stress is a way to keep people divided. To override this strategy of the enemy, stewardship must be taught and practiced.

4
Satan's Military Organizational Structure

¹He who dwells in the secret place of the Most High
Shall abide under the shadow of the Almighty.
² I will say of the Lord, "*He is* my refuge and my fortress;
My God, in Him I will trust." ³ Surely He shall deliver you from the snare of the [a] fowler
And from the perilous pestilence.

Psalm 91

The dark world is an organization and sophisticated system. It is true, the devil creates havoc in the earth. However, the destruction that he creates is not outside of the infrastructure that he has instituted. Satan's kingdom has rankings and structure. In his kingdom, nothing just happens without strategic planning. Everything that he authorizes is calculated for maximum results. Ephesians 6 vs 12 says, "For we wrestle not against flesh and blood, but against principalities, against powers, against the rulers of the darkness of this world, against spiritual wickedness in high places." The inclusions in this verse provide some insight into the infrastructure of Satan's kingdom. Fr. Gabriele Amorth says, "Satan, the most beautiful of all the angels, being aware of his extreme intelligence, rebelled at the idea of being subjected to someone."[1] Therefore, because of being banished from heaven, he mirrored the structure of the heavens and instituted in his kingdom.

We are in war! The battle ground is the will of man. Subsequently, for Satan to press his agenda as an opposing force of God, he uses his infrastructure to challenge the will of man. Satan's kingdom is organized. The has roles and functions for each area of his personnel. He uses a military strategy to gather intelligence and enforce his agenda on the earth. The sections of Satan's kingdom are set up as follows: General, Officers, Non-Commissioned Officers, and Enlisted Personnel.

ROLES AND FUNCTIONS

The General

Satan is the *General*. He is the one who controls and dictates the kingdom. He is recognized and acknowledged by three names: Satan, Devil, Prince of the Air. Ephesians 2 vs 2 says, "Wherein in time past ye walked according to the course of this world, according to the prince of the power of the air, the spirit that now worketh in the children of disobedience:" The Greek word for prince is "árchōn ἄρχων, which means a first (in rank or power):—chief (ruler), magistrate, prince, ruler."[1] As the archon, he governs the earth and manages the dark world. This authority was given to him in Revelation 12 vs 9, "And the great dragon was cast out, that old serpent, called the Devil, and Satan, which deceiveth the whole world: he was cast out into the earth, and his angels were cast out with him." When he was cast to the earth, this was the institution of his kingdom. If would seem as though the angels would be his officers, however, there is another power that stands ahead of the angels in the dark world.

Officers

Ephesians 6 vs 12 says, "For we wrestle not against flesh and blood, but against principalities, against powers, against the rulers of the darkness of this world, against spiritual wickedness in high places." Principalities in the Greek ἀρχή **arché,** (properly abstract) a commencement, or (concretely) chief (in various applications of order, time, place, or rank): —beginning, corner, (at the, the) first (estate), magistrate, power, principality, principle, rule.[2] Satan establishes principalities as chief angels in regions. These angels work to keep strongholds in place over regions. Also, they create war against heavenly angels that are assigned to release blessings to the earth. Many principalities do not have names, but other religions recognize other God's. The names of demons are used by those in Satanic or occultic practices for the purpose of connecting with ancient forces that are historical in the dark world.

Demonic officers can be officiators of oppression, plagues, and/or pandemics. They do not initiate these war tactics on their own. The command is released by the chief angel (Satan), then spiritual workers will engage with demons and will facilitate his command. Paul says in Romans 8 vs 38, "For I am persuaded, that neither death, nor life, nor angels, nor principalities, nor powers, nor things present, nor things to come." Paul recognizes the opposing force of principalities and communicates in this chapter that he is fully persuaded and convinced about Christ in his life. Strongholds must be torn or broken down.

These officers can place high levels of resistance in society. For example, you can have a community that is extremely poverty stricken. Children can grow up in that community and become educated. They can start a career and raise a family. However, in most cases, when the person begins to advance their life, they will be forced to relocate to a place that is more conducive to seeing their dreams actualized. When the stronghold is active in a region that is full of poverty, the enemy will perpetuate it to keep the people's minds captive.

Most of the time, poverty-stricken communities are willing to receive aid or assistance from outsiders. However, the people at large will resist any empowerment or training that is offered to show them their potential. Strongholds are not concerned about controlling or possessing one person, they are more interested in dominating systems, families, nations, and/or regions.

I remember my first trip to Cagayan de Oro, Philippines. As the airplane was flying from Manila to CDO, when we were approaching Mindanao the clouds in the sky changed. It was evident that we crossed into a different climate and region. On the grounds of Cagayan de Oro in city proper and other places, the people were friendly, however, the lifestyles chosen by some of the people were unique. Because of overcrowding and economic challenges, there are many things that remain present in the region that are designed to keep the economy poverty driven. In this city, there are many retail malls. Being an outsider, it would appear as though the economy is doing well for malls to be built with 4 to 5 levels to them. But this is a camouflage of the reality of individuals daily lifestyles in the Cagayan de Oro.

Homelessness is a huge factor in CDO. There are children being born and left on the street becoming orphans because of abandonment. Amongst many other concerns from the citizens, the reality of the stronghold that resides over that region is also a byproduct of what is happening in that region of the earth.

During another visit, I travelled to Iligan City. To get to the city, you had to pass through Marawi. This area is highly concentrated by Muslims and known to harbor Islamic extremist (Isis). This time, while travelling to Iligan City for revival, war broke out in Marawi between Islamic extremist and Filipino military. Isis formed a stronghold in the city of Marawi. Strongholds do not practice rules of engagement for war.

Strongholds will use human barricades such as family, friends, legislators, superiors, employers, sexuality, and more to keep Satan's agenda present and active in the earth. In John Howard Yoder's review of the 'Total War' concept, he references the Vatican Council II *Gaudium et Spes* (The Church in the Modern World) response to war; he says, "Any act of war aimed indiscriminately at the destruction of entire cities or of extensive areas along with their population is a crime against God and man himself. It merits unequivocal and unhesitating condemnation."[4] Satan's agenda includes tormenting lives individually and corporately.

Israel faced Jericho in the book of Joshua. Jericho was a stronghold, that was fortified. The bible recants that story by sharing, nothing was going out and nothing was coming in, however, God ordained for Israel to occupy the place of the stronghold. Through their obedience, the benefited from the power of God breaking the stronghold. For strongholds to remain a force of opposition, they must engage other members of Satan's infrastructure. Engaging demonic angels and satanic practices are ways strongholds intertwine themselves in regions.

Non-Commissioned Officers (NCO)

The traditional understanding of a non-commissioned officer is when a person is given more responsibility without having the commissioned authority. In Satan's kingdom his non-commissioned officers are his angels. Demonic Angels can manifest themselves in the form of spirits and conditions. There are many names that can be associated with the non-commissioned officers which we recognize as demonic spirits. Adrian Rogers says, "The devil is now the lord of these fallen angels, and together they form a demonized, organized, and mobilized power of satanic wicknedess."[3] These angels are infamous for assisting in terrorizing the world. Frank and Ida Mae Hammond say, "Demons are evil personalities. They are spirit beings. They are the enemies of God and man. Their objectives in human beings are to temp, deceive, accuse, condemn, pressure, defile, resist, oppose, control, steal, afflict, kill and destroy."[5] These angels of the devil are committed to the mission of Satan.

1 Peter 5 vs 8 informs us that the devil looks for prey to devour. He uses a combination of things to demonstrate his power over mankind. The role of the demonic angels is to remain in alignment with Satan's agenda. Their function includes occupying space in the lives of humans. Demonic possession is deeper than someone having panic or anxiety attacks. Also, it is more complex than it being the summation of a person experiencing trauma in their life. We must wage war against Satan's kingdom. Deliverance cannot not be an attribute of the modern church if there is disbelief in demonic angels' ability to possess an individual. Matthew 10 vs 1 says, "And when he had called unto him his twelve disciples, he gave them power against unclean spirits, to cast them out, and to heal all manner of sickness and all manner of disease." Because Jesus gave his disciples this power, deliverance still has purpose in the lives of people and in the modern church.

The term 'spiritual warfare' is a common term used in charismatic ministry. It is "a term used to describe conflict and intangible infliction and assaults that emanate from, and take place in, the invisible spheres of creation."[6] In Satan's infrastructure, it is the role and responsibility of demonic angels and those he has enlisted to combine their efforts to create battlegrounds for war. The battleground for spiritual battles extends beyond the war within a person's mind. Isaiah 23 vs 6 says, "Thou will keep him in perfect peace whose mind is stayed on thee: because he trusteth in thee." Therefore, the enemy does not only initiate the mind of man as the only battleground for war. He uses anything that will affect human life and trust in God to create a battleground to initiate war.

The theory of the battlefield being in the mind, and the outcome of the war being mental illness begins with philosopher Sigmund Freud. Jeffrey Russell says,

> "Sigmund Freud took religion as a mere psychological phenomenon who origins and nature can be not only explained but explained away. --- Freud developed a diabology whose central point was that "the Devil is clearly nothing other than the personification of repressed, unconscious drives. Because the Evil One traditionally took on many shaped and forms, Feud was able to identify him with an equally diverse number of mental disorders."[7]

The rules of engagement for demonic angels are not designed to only attack the mind. In Mark chapter 5, Jesus encounters a man who lives in the country of the Gadarenes, and he has made his residence among graves. Jesus delivered this man by casting an evil spirit out of the man. The same man that could not be restrained by anyone or anything was now freed from his inner struggle.

Evil spirits occupy objects, but the objects are not the evil spirit. For example, there is no such thing as a "cigarette demon or alcohol demon." Cigarettes and alcohol are products that can be used in substance abuse, and embraced by a person to suppress nature feelings, etc. However, the spirit of bondage or addiction is what could be manifesting in the life of the person.

> Romans 8:15 says, "For ye have not received the spirit of bondage again to fear; but ye have received the Spirit of adoption, whereby we cry, Abba, Father."

When a person is possessed, it can alter their behavior, perception, physical appearance, and their morale. Frank and Ida May Hammond say there are seven common symptoms present in a person's life when discerning if deliverance is needed. The symptoms are emotional problems, mental problems, speech problems, sex problems, addictions, physical infirmities, and/or religious error. These symptoms are not limited to or the only ways to identify if a person needs deliverance. However, knowing that the enemy will use anything against a person or family to get his agenda across. It is important to note that deliverance should be coupled with salvation or an introduction to Christ. Deliverance is not designed to free people from their inner struggle, so that they can reset their lives and continue living life vicariously.

The difference between nonbelievers and believers engaging in spiritual battles. Because of the presence of the Holy Spirit, believers will experience a conviction within their soul when they have done anything contrary to the character of Christ. The conviction of Christ is evidence that the individual is still connected to the Father. However, the enemy will use condemnation against the believer as a wall to keep them in bondage. Rather than the believer accepting the grace of God, he/she will condemn themselves or embrace the condemnation of others and fail to accept God's forgiveness towards them. Believers cannot be possessed by evil spirits until they totally forsake their conviction in Christ. Therefore, Satan employs different concepts, tactics, and personnel to initiate battles in the life of people to keep society bound or disconnected from true vine in Christ.

ENLISTED MILITARY PERSONNEL

Ephesians 6 vs 12 mentions that we will also war against rulers of the darkness of this world and against spiritual wickedness in high places. Satan uses human beings in strategic places to perpetuate his agenda in earth against mankind. He gives satanic military orders to men and women to carry out his agenda. He can persuade people from all walks of life to initiate his plans. If a person's heart is not committed to God, neither are they concerned about living their lives with a Christian conviction, Satan will consider that person as a candidate to carry out his plan. Working for Satan is not usually a voluntary call. It is not uncommon for people who are employed by the devil to have experienced extreme traumatic experiences in their life. In other instances, some people have been indoctrinated into to a lifestyle of practicing various forms of witchcraft. In the structure of Satan's kingdom, it is common for him to use various spiritual workers. He will use diviners, medium workers, satanic priest, cults, and occultic practices strategically.

When Satan employs these men and women around the world, they have different names but the same agenda. When the battle has been initiated in certain communities, they only recognize spiritual workers and diviners according to their specific cultural experience. Generally, the world is accustomed to evil being attributed to Satan (the Devil) as the officiator. Therefore, in effort to keep his kingdom moving in the earth, he has diversified his identity within communities globally. Traditionally, rulers of darkness of this world originated out of Africa. The reason is because of Africa being the origin of mankind. However, the devil has not limited his terrorizing of communities to the continent of Africa. Throughout time, occultic practice has spanned around the world. John S Mbiti says, "Every village in Africa has a medicine-man within reach, and he is the friend of the community. He is accessible to everybody and at almost all times and comes into the picture at many points in individual and community life."[8] The approach that John Mbiti takes in his book is a desired approach of Satan in communities around the world. It is the plot of Satan for mankind to not see his personnel as a threat to society.

In the modern day, Satan has different names around the world. As I travel globally, I have noticed how the enemy uses spiritual wickedness in high places and creates allegiances with mankind in places of poverty. He accomplishes this by the commitment of people to carry out his will. Here is a list of common names used to describe a spiritual worker in communities abroad:

- Obeah Man - Jamaica

- Stregoneria – Italy

- Tambalan, Quack Doctor – Philippines

- MGanga – Kenya

- Mchawi – Tanzania

- Vrăjitoare/Vrăjitor – Romania

- Bruja/Brujo – Centra -South America

- Witch, Witchdoctor, Warlock, Root Worker – United States

The term witchcraft is seen as a negative word in non-Christian communities. However, within Christian communities, these spiritual workers are seen more so as the agents of the devil. In Acts chapter 16, there is a story about young girl who was possessed by the spirit of divination who worked as a soothsayer. A soothsayer is equivalent to a fortune teller. She was good at what she did because her owners profited much from her practice. She tormented Paul and Silas by mocking them, therefore, this initiated her deliverance through Paul. Adrian Rogers says, "Satan will marshal all the forces of hell and the demons of darkness to keep you in ignorance about your Kingdom Authority. Satan wants to deceive you into thinking that victory is impossible---even if you are swimming in an ocean of potential blessing!"[9] The enlisted personnel of Satan's kingdom are designed to persuade people against embracing the resurrecting power of God.

He also uses occultic practices to contradict the Christian experience. Cults have been used to practice a type of Christianity while alienating itself from truths about Christian heritage. Cults can be religious but heretical. Moreover, Satanic priest will be officiators within the Satanic religion. Jeffrey Russell says, "The essential function of Satan in the New Testament is to obstruct the kingdom of God as long and as thoroughly as he can."[10] Satan institutes this plan in the earth by defusing his organizational chart into "Demonic Companies and Special Units" in his infrastructure.

5
Military Infrastructure of the Devil's Kingdom

⁶ God has spoken in His holiness:
"I will rejoice;
I will divide Shechem
And measure out the Valley of Succoth.
⁷ Gilead *is* Mine, and Manasseh *is* Mine;
Ephraim also *is* the [c]helmet for My head;
Judah *is* My lawgiver.
⁸ Moab *is* My washpot;
Over Edom I will cast My shoe;
Philistia, shout in triumph because of Me."

Psalm 60

Spiritual Warfare

A term used to describe conflict and intangible infliction and assaults that emanate from, and take place in, the invisible spheres of creation. It is centered on God's invisible creatures battling with the prayers of His saints, members of the church of Jesus Christ, on earth. New Creation believer prayers, opposition, envy, kingdom infighting, and carnal resistance can also inspire spiritual warfare. 2 Corinthians 10:4[1]

In Satan's kingdom, the roles and functions of his army personnel perpetuates his agenda in the earth. Even though his kingdom has a hierarchical structure, one role or function is not more important than the other. Therefore, he continues to terrorize the earth by working his detailed infrastructure. Within his army, there are demonic companies and special units just as a military force is constructed, today. However, the enemy camouflages himself as a strategic tactic to push his agenda. Understanding how his kingdom is structure will provide clarity of how he employs territorial demons, strongholds, demonic angels, spiritual workers, heresy, and more.

The division of the dark world that is under Satan's jurisdiction is governed by his army. Satan's army does not overthrow God's Kingdom, but it does war against the heavens and God's redemptive and resurrection power for mankind. Revelation 12 vs 7-10 describes this type of engagement. "[7] And there were war in heaven: Michael and his angels fought against the dragon; and the dragon fought and his angels, [8] And prevailed not; neither was their place found any more in heaven. [9] And the great dragon was cast out, that old serpent, called the Devil, and Satan, which deceiveth the whole world: he was cast out into the earth, and his angels were cast out with him." The Greek word for war is πόλεμος pólemos which means warfare, a battle, fight, or war. Warfare against the believer has several agendas in hopes of accomplishing one goal by Satan.

In Revelation, the demonic angels that waged war against the heaven operated in a rebellion under the leadership of the Devil with intent to overthrow the heavens. Satan's strategic plan was to use persuasion and manipulation to initiate this agenda. Today,

Satan uses his army to continue waging war. However, the war is not a battle of the heavens, but the war happens in the cosmos and within the earth. In the cosmos, angelic beings continue to fight each other.

In Daniel chapter 10, he describes an encounter where his angle was at war for 21 days. The enemy continues to use this strategy against mankind in hopes of getting influencers and people to sway from their truth. He does not care if we know the truth, he just does not want anyone to be convicted by the truth. When the serpent interacts with the woman in Genesis 3, his uses persuasion and manipulation against the woman to get her to second guess herself about the truth. He says in vs 3-4, "⁴ And the serpent said unto the woman, Ye shall not surely die: ⁵ For God doth know that in the day ye eat thereof, then your eyes shall be opened, and ye shall be as gods, knowing good and evil." He continues to use this tactic within his army. When a person is broken by Satan's manipulation, then he is less likely to resist any of the additional attacks and schemes.

He uses things that he knows will entice the believer when manipulation and persuasion is in effect. Every aspect of his army will employ this tactic as they attempt to carry out the plan of the enemy. James 1 vs 14-15 says, "¹⁴ But each one is tempted when he is drawn away by his own desires and enticed. ¹⁵ Then, when desire has conceived, it gives birth to sin; and sin, when it is full-grown, brings forth death." Satan's army is given intel about mankind, societies, kingdoms, and governments.

Some of his regime carry out some assignments by tempting mankind with desire. When mankind is tempted by desire or self-gratification it could possibly cause them to live a religious life but not a Christian life by conviction. Spiritual warfare always involves rules of, that includes, but is not limited to art and strategy to war. The are no treaties or alliances, however, allegiance is expected. The war that the enemy creates against the believer is because of their allegiance to God and their commitment to Christian convictions. The war is calculated, based on weaponry, strategy, endurance, emotional stability, and a healthy psyche. 2 Corinthians vs 4 says, "⁴ (For the weapons of our warfare are not carnal, but mighty through God to the pulling down of strong holds;)" When believers engage in spiritual battles, they must remain in constant dialogue with the Holy Spirit that they may not respond to a spiritual battle with a carnal response.

It must be noted, when a person is engaged in war, that fatigue is a byproduct of war. Ralph D. Sawyer says, "When employing them in battle, a victory that is long in coming will blunt their weapons and dampen their ardor. --- When the weapons have grown dull and spirits depressed, when our strength has been extended and resources consumed, then the feudal lords will take advantage of our exhaustion to arise."2 The enemy knows that believers do not fight well when they are tired. People are less likely to resist when they are exhausted. Therefore, Satan will use demonic angels to terrorize the mind of people.

BRIGADE

A military brigade is a unit consisting of a variable number of combat battalions or regiments; a group of persons organized for a specific purpose. Satan's brigade is his unit of demonic angels. The functions of the angels are to help Satan remain a controlling force in the orchestration and implementation of evil in the earth. Demonic angels can also be assigned to initiate some natural disasters. All natural disasters are not natural, some storms have destroyed cities and the lives of people.

Demonic angels can target families and generations. If they can keep a family bound and negating their kingdom authority, their assignment is being fulfilled. There was a time I was in the Philippines preaching revival. In this revival, a young adult in her early twenties was present. During the altar ministry, this young adult mentioned to a youth leader that she wanted to relinquish her power. They brought the young adult to me during this moment. Quickly, I was able to assess that she was wearing a charm from a spell caster. This charm is supposed to keep the person away from evil or evil things happening to them. However, she was not informed that the charm does not keep you away from Jesus. In relationship to demonic angels terrorizing families, when the charm was removed, three of her family members came to the altar for prayer and salvation. On that day a four-person family changed their life and belief system. Satan's brigade encompasses the function of all the military components under his command.

BATTALION

A *Battalion* is one of the military components in Satan's army. A battalion is an army unit typically having a headquarters and two or more companies, batteries, or similar number. Satan's battalion involves demonic terrorism. He institutes territorial demons to carry out global functions and regional assignments. Within the battalion there will be angels, occults, spiritual workers, and satanic priest that will be planted in regions who agree with Satan's agenda. They will all work together in times and seasons to carry out their individual assignments in efforts of accomplishing Satan's agenda.

Territorial Demons are different from strongholds because they are identified by name. Spiritual workers who practice spiritual wickedness are taught the name of these demons by heritage and practice. Therefore, these demons sit in high places within the cosmos waiting to be acknowledged. Satan uses people like Anton Szandor LaVey to create opposition against Christian principles and the hope that people have in Christ. In Satan's regime, Anton would fall under the command of regional assignments. However, because the earth is Satan's domain, there are global assignments that he employs against mankind worldwide.

Anton Szandor LaVey

He led an American occult and called himself the high priest. He was known for his rection his rejection of traditional Christianity. He founded the church of Satan in San Francisco, CA. He published *The Satanic Bible*, teaching people the rituals and beliefs of his church. He believed that traditional religions were filled with hypocrisy. He was formerly known as a church musician as a teenager. He taught his followers to obey the law and that they could indulge in the pleasures of life because it is a benefit to living.[3]

The global functions of territorial demons can include placing plagues within communities, racial disharmony, classism and tribalism, economic disparities, and economic deficiency, etc. Controlling communities and influencing societies to discredit God and His ability. Therefore, the devil continues to employ strategic assignment in regions. Tailoring specific strongholds within in regions can affect the economy, quality of life, education, crime, and culture. Therefore, Satan deploys strongholds as a company within the *Battalion*.

A *Company* is a subdivision of military regiment or battalion that constitutes the lowest administrative unit, made up of at least two platoons. Satan administers his plan using "strongholds." Derek Prince says, "If you want to be successful in any given situation, you must discover who or what the satanic "strongman" is over that situation. --- But the principle is to first bind the strong man --- then set his captives free and recover what was lost."[4] Strongmen are used to fortify the enemy's plans, as well as keep things instituted throughout generations.

Mark 3 vs 27 says, "No man can enter into a strong man's house, and spoil his goods, except he will first bind the strong man; and then he will spoil his house." It is impossible to enter a region where a strong man is planted not knowing his characteristic, purpose, or territory. When I am identifying the strongman of a region, I will study and explore the region unannounced. Every strong man will release characteristics of their strongholds in due time. Demonic possession of a person requires the evil spirit to be cast out. Binding the strongman is an elevated fight. The fight is elevated because of the level of authority that has been given to them in the dark world of Satan's army. Therefore, the enemy reinforces the stronghold by commanding and releasing platoons to carry out his plan on the ground.

PLATOON

A *Platoon* is a subdivision of a company of troops consisting of two or more squads or sections usually commanded by a lieutenant. This small division of Satan's kingdom is carried out by footmen who are influencers. They manipulate kingdoms, governments, systems, and groves of people. From occultic leaders to religious extremist, Satan strategically place these people in positions of influence. He does this to offset society's ability to progress together, living in harmony, and ultimately seeing Jesus Christ as savior of the world.

Revelation 11 vs 15 says, "And the seventh angel sounded; and there were great voices in heaven, saying, "The kingdoms of this world are become the kingdoms of our Lord, and of his Christ; and he shall reign for ever and ever." The kingdoms of this world are always in opposition with the Kingdom of God. This verse is not referring to the carnal thinking of man, but it is talking more about the provision and expectation of the world. The does not want mankind to believe in the provisions of God. Therefore, Satan's agents try their best to deceive and control man's thinking. The platoon's job is to infiltrate families and sway cultures away from God.

Spiritual wickedness in high places can include legislators and law makers. The enemy will initiate laws to continue to perpetuate his agenda to frustrate believers' movement in spiritual war. In 1 Timothy 1 vs 18, Paul tells Timothy to remain faithful to the prophecies spoken that he might wage a good warfare. Satan knows that believers build their trust on the word of God. Therefore, he compounds his efforts with evil workers, actions, and deeds. He uses a squadron of Spiritual workers with specific assignments.

SQUADRON

A *Squadron* is an armored cavalry unit subordinate to a regiment and consisting of two or more troops. Satan uses squadron in the form of spiritual workers. In today's time, he uses occultism to carry out assignments in the earth. Occultism is the study of supernatural power and the belief in occult powers and the possibility of bringing them under human control. In this day in time, there are pastors, and that practice occult practices in their private life. When Satan has released a squadron to keep people bound, specific squadrons can be effective in keeping people powerless and hopeless. I remember a time when I was travelling abroad, I encountered people who were affected by pastors who practiced witchcraft. These kinds of pastors were used by Satan to carry out Satan's plan of deception and religious lawlessness.

Frank and Ida Mae Hammond said, "Satan has a method---a settled plan---to conquer each one of us, along with our family, church, community and nation."[5] When Satan deploys smaller teams, he is able to terrorize mankind more directly and intently. In Ephesians 6, Paul mentions that we ware against rulers of darkness of this world. Spiritual workers establish businesses in communities where their services will be needed. This implementation is done strategically to lessen the threat of these services. Services such as fortune-telling, psychics, palm reading, terror card reading, astrology, cosmic stones, etc. The squadrons can be broken down into teams. The squadrons and the teams are used most in effecting the quality of life for mankind.

TEAMS

Teams are a group of people organized to work together. Satan uses teams intertwined with squadrons depending on the specific cause and effect he is desires to accomplish. Father Gabriele Amorth says, "The most significant forms of occultism are magic, astrology, fortune-telling, and or spiritism. At its base is the belief in the existence of spiritual forces that cannot be experienced through one's external senses (i.e., touch, sight, and so forth); therefore, they are esoteric or hidden."[6] Terrorizing people, families, and communities require strategic planning and consistent persecution. Through these mediums and others, the Devil does all that he can to keep mankind in hopeless situations.

2 Timothy 3 vs 5 says, "Having a form of godliness, but denying the power thereof: from such turn away." The enemy does not mind if people will reverence God by acknowledging His ability, however, his goal is to destroy the name of God in the hearts and mind of people. Through teams we can see the initiation of a social gospel

in a social age. Denying the true gospel in a social age will alienate men from believing in righteous living.

The infrastructure of the dark world is strategically and systemically implemented in Satan's agenda. There is a reason why all these areas are used by Satan. Many people will give more creditability to astrology and numerology in Christian contexts than those that believe in the truth of God. Because Satan has been infamous in deploying his assignments among mankind that people will acknowledge the power of agents in the dark world while discrediting the power of the gifts of God. The war is an ongoing battle until Jesus returns. Until Jesus returns, it is important to know the rules of engagement and demonic concepts of war when engaging in spiritual battles.

6
Rules of Engagement

¹Do not fret because of evildoers, Nor be envious of the workers of iniquity.
²For they shall soon be cut down like the grass,
And wither as the green herb.

³Trust in the LORD, and do good;
Dwell in the land, and feed on His faithfulness.

Psalm 37

Declaring war on the enemy is a strategic process. There is more required to declaring war on the Devil than creating daily affirmations or declarations. When declaring war, there are rules for engagement. Understanding the rules for engagement lessens the chances of becoming a prisoner of war in spiritual battles or a severely wounded warrior because of spiritual battles. Spiritual battles are common, however, the preparation for spiritual battles is not as common. In Matthew 17, there is a story of a certain man bringing his son to Jesus to be delivered. After the deliverance, his disciples asked why they could not cast out the evil spirit. Jesus replies in verses 20-21 by saying, "[20] And Jesus said unto them, Because of your unbelief: for verily I say unto you, if ye have faith as a grain of mustard seed, ye shall say unto this mountain, remove hence to yonder place; and it shall remove; and nothing shall be impossible unto you. [21] Howbeit this kind goeth not out but by prayer and fasting." The foundation of the rules of engagement requires you to prepare spiritually.

Daily devotion and a good practice of spiritual formation are basic practices for preparation for engagement. Engaging in spiritual battles also requires one to understand what level of war that they are engaging. Spiritual battles are not like acts of war in the earth. In the earth, there will be military against military, people against people, or kingdoms against kingdoms. In spiritual battles, there will never be a battle against Satan's kingdom in totality. That battle will happen when Christ returns in the second coming. Until then, based on the persons level of maturity and effectiveness in the kingdom of God, it will determine the level of war that a person will experience. James 3 vs 15 says, "This wisdom descendeth not from above, but is earthly, sensual, devilish." In this verse, James is referring to envy and strife. He identifies that there are three levels of manifestation when engaging in this kind of battle. The first level of demonic effect is within the dimensions of the earth, the second level is within human's inner struggle, and the third level is demonic influence. Derek Prince says, "that become to earthly causes men to lose vision of eternity, becoming soulish causes people to become self-centered and egocentric, and the demonic is the avenue in which demons infiltrate the church."[1]

Engaging in a spiritual battle must include assessing what force you are encountering. You must discern if the force territorial, regional, communal, governmental, legislative, cultural, familial, or personal. There are rules of preparation when engaging each mode of attack from the enemy. The enemy will attack the flesh of man. However, the flesh includes more than a attack on the five senses of man. He will launch an attack through those five senses, but he is does not limit the attack to the five senses. There is a wide held belief that the greatest battlefield is within the mind. Romans 12 vs 15 says, "And be not conformed to this world: but be ye transformed by the renewing of your mind, that ye may prove what is that good, and acceptable, and perfect, will of God." Through this verse the concept of the mind being the battlefield is created. However, the enemy knows the complication with this type of thinking in the modern world. Simply because in Greco-Roman times, the term "mind" had a deeper meaning than a notion of how we think.

The Greek word for mind is **νοῦς noûs,** which means the intellect, i.e., mind (divine or human; in thought, feeling, or will); by implication, meaning: —mind.[2] In Greek thought the mind is shaped by culture, experiences, religion, education, age, of the times. A person's worldview is shaped by their mind. In addition to that, they also believed that the mind was an interpretation of the condition of the soul. The ultimate battleground is within the heart of the believer and in the soul of the unbeliever. This is important because when men are saved by grace, they are not saved by their mind, neither do they repent in their mind. The verse that is commonly used to invite people into this inheritance with Christ is Romans 10 vs 9-10. Which says, "[9] That if thou shalt confess with thy mouth the Lord Jesus, and shalt believe in thine heart that God hath raised him from the dead, thou shalt be saved. [10] For with the heart man believeth unto righteousness; and with the mouth confession is made unto salvation." Rules of engagement for initiating a battle with the enemy should begin with understanding the following: 1. the terror against your trust in God. 2. the intentional conflict brought against your confession.

Being an optimistic person does not mean a person does not have a challenge within their soul or choose to live their life as a believer in Christ. The enemy's rule for engagement begins with his purpose to continue perpetuating his agenda against the plan of God for mankind. 1 Peter 5 vs 8 talks about the enemy being a roaring lion. In the attributes of a lion, they will attack anything that they feel is threatening their den. The enemy takes on the same nature, he will create an offensive attack intentionally against anyone who is threatening his kingdom. Threatening Satan's kingdom can include creating programs that increase the welfare of mankind, preaching and teaching people the gospel of Jesus Christ, practicing forgiveness and other fruits of the spirit. He does not want the earth to live in harmony with God and peace with each other. Remaining a terrorist to the Christian experience helps him in trying to delegitimize the truth of the power of Christ's resurrection.

When Satan was banished to the earth becoming the prince of the air, he and his angels declared war against the heavens and the earth. Satan initiated this war intentionally. He wars against mankind because of man's ability to live beyond human will and desire and seek a higher calling through Christ Jesus. In his initiative to seek for those whom he can devour, he takes on prisoners of war through a variety of ways. Before examining the ways that Satan takes prisoners of war, I must first be truthful about Satan's perspective of death. He does not see death as imprisonment to the Christian believer. The early church in the 1st -4th century grew in part because of martyrs. Satan does not want to take the life of a Christian if their death is going to advance the kingdom of God. The preferred method of causing people to be prisoners of war is by causing their life to not match their confession. The strategy of the devil is to use a combination of traumatic experiences, illnesses, family challenges, economic deficiency, emotional disturbances, self-induced afflictions, character assassination, deception, and more. Combining many initiatives leverages Satan's attack against mankind. He does not expect many people to have the fortitude that Job demonstrated when he was attack. In the story of Job, God solicited Job to be tried of Satan. Through these series of trials, Job experienced many challenges and loses. He lost his economic status, his family, his health, and his respect. As a result of this challenges, Job was interrogated by his friends. Their interrogation questioned Jobs relationship with God because the region knew that Job was an upright and just man. Therefore, it was hard to comprehend how tragedy would attack his life to that degree.

When the enemy imprisons a person, they will live their lives within the confine and restraints that he (Satan) has created for them. The confinement is designed to restrict the believer's belief in God. Satan uses extreme tactics throughout the bible as a sign of his hatred of those being sent or used of God. Daniel was thrown in the lion's den as capital punishment for not obeying the kings decree to worship Baal. His friends were given pagan names (Shadrach, Meshach, Abednego) to disassociated them from YWHW, ultimately, there punishment was to enter a furnace that was seven times hotter than the original heat. Christ received punishment and was crucified. In each of these instances, Satan's hope was that people would stop believing in God. Unfortunately, he continues to use this tactic against believers today. Because God, knows the intent of the enemy, He encourages us in 2 Timothy 2 vs 3-5 by telling us to endure the hardship as good soldiers.

Spiritual battles are designed to affect your perspective, delay your time, disrupt your focus, and ignite fear in the heart of the person. Father Gabriele Amorth says, "We are all victims of temptation, but only some are victims of the extraordinary action of Satan, but never through their own fault; therefore, they are not morally responsible. Temptation assaults us each holy day."[3] There are times when the believer can feel like they are in a whirlwind. Many times, the believer will try to ignore the whirlwind or claim it to be something else as result of their negligence or lack of attention, unknowingly to the believer. The reason Satan employs this scheme is because, when the believer opts out of including God in their situation, they leave themselves open to responding to life based on their intuition or superstition.

Satan desires to imprison with sin. He knows that sin separates the person from God, but he camouflages the sinful nature of man. Tatha Wiley says, "Sin is not the result of the lack of "good choice" or "good moral impulse.""[4] The impact of sin causes "good choice" to be overridden immoral imprecation. Sin awakens a desire that makes the choice irresistible. Sin is the result of an action that separates man from God. The human choice is an important element in the evidence of sin. Human choice is different from divine will. The divine will of God in totally controlled by Him, and humans can choose to embrace the divine will or follow human will. Human error segregates man from God. Human error is not just an action of misjudgment. The error is directly applied to God's expectation of mankind. Sin is not so evasive that it applies to all human error. For example, making a poor choice of directions to go to the grocery store is not associated with the human error that is consequential of sin. For human error to become a violation against God, then there must be an overshadowing foreknowledge of God's response to sin.

Sin is not just an element that exposes behavioral inconsistencies with mankind. Sin is more than just being an offense towards God. Moreover, sin is the known and self-recognition of failure within one-self. Self has the capacity whether intentionally or unintentionally to offend God. In John Hannah's work, he mentions to truly understand sin that we must understand the redemptive nature of God.[5] All through the ages, Sin has carried is origin through the failure of Adam.

Yes, Adam failed however, it was the element that was needed to introduce liberation of self into the world. We are encompassed of many emotions; therefore, Kierkegaard saw the human nature as relative to the possibility of human error.[6]

Being a prisoner to sin is one of Satan's ways of keeping the believer from experiencing the promises of God. The war that men experience is not just external. Paul mentions the inner war raging within himself. Romans 7 vs 23 says, "But I see another law in my members, warring against the law of my mind, and bringing me into captivity to the law of sin which is in my members." The war inside begins with the inner struggle of man. Satan strategizes and plans his attacks against mankind. When a person is attacked by Satan, in most cases there is a dualistic feud that has been initiated with the purpose to keep the person imbalanced. The feud can be the inward struggle to rationalize life and the outward critique of others that can further complicate one's ability to reason.

3 John 1 vs 2 says, "Beloved, I wish above all things that thou mayest prosper and be in health, even as thy soul prospereth." When the enemy wages war against the soul, he has determined to impact a person's perception of themselves. Many people will spend time trying to find the imperfections in their soul when trying to achieve the prosperity referred to in 3 John 1. The perfection is in only found in the Lord. However, God has given man the Holy Spirit as an advocate. The work of the Holy Spirit walks alongside man and God simultaneously. Part of the work of the Holy Spirit is to intercede on behalf of the believer. Romans 8 vs 26, "Likewise the Spirit also helpeth our infirmities: for we know not what we should pray for as we ought: but the Spirit itself maketh intercession for us with groanings which cannot be uttered." In acts of war, the enemy's agenda is to try to make the scripture become null and void to them that believe.

Satan's purpose for waging war also includes his intent for our eschatological views on the end-times to be altered. He knows that the end will come, therefore, he knows that all believers will be judged by God and the heavenly council. Moreover, he intently creates war to jeopardize a person's pursuit of eternal rest in the heavens. Father Gabriele Amorth says, "The one who dies in mortal sin without repenting goes to hell; in an impenitent way, he has not loved. It is not God who predestines a soul to hell; the soul chooses it with the way [the person] has lived his life."[7] Ultimately the devil wants as many as possible to be confused about the end of life. Eternal damnation is a truth about the Christian experience. Men are not measured by their good works alone.

Satan wages war on the believer knowing that a believer does not enter eternal grace by good merits alone. God is concerned about the heart of man being reconciled with him. The pre-requisite for reconciliation with God is repentance. Christianity is not a merit-based religion; however, the enemy will create war that will cause people to base their love for Christ on merit and deeds. In the book of Revelation, John is instructed to write a letter to the angel of the church in Smyrna. In his discourse to the church, he mentions their condition, however, God gives a response to their conditions in Revelation 2 vs 9-10. "[9] I know thy works, and tribulation, and poverty, (but thou art rich) and I know the blasphemy of them which say they are Jews, and are not, but are the synagogue of Satan. [10] Fear none of those things which thou shalt suffer: behold, the devil shall cast some of you into prison, that ye may be tried; and ye shall have tribulation ten days: be thou faithful unto death, and I will give thee a crown of life."

The passage in Revelation is evidence that exposes the continued plans of Satan. He desires that we be imprisoned and experience tribulation unto death. Escaping the traps of the enemy requires you to know your kingdom authority. Satan does not want anyone to know their God given power over Satan. Luke 10 vs 18-19 says, "[18] And he said unto them, I beheld Satan as lightning fall from heaven. [19] Behold, I give unto you power to tread on serpents and scorpions, and over all the power of the enemy: and nothing shall by any means hurt you." Satan knows this power has been given unto man, therefore, the war that he creates is designed for people to not walk in that power. Adrian Rogers says, "As believers, we should walk on conquered ground. Stake your claim of faith on the promises of God. And do as Winston Churchill once said, "Never give in, never give in, never, never, never, never.""[8] The key to navigating through the battle ground with Satan is to remain confident in God. Learn to develop in the places of battle.

Winning the battle is not about how many people that you have supporting you in the battle. In Matthew 18 vs 20, Jesus informs that disciples that if two-three people are gathering in His name, he guarantees being in the midst of them. Therefore, when the enemy wages war, he diversifies his army by using different war concepts in the battle. Diversifying his concepts gives him the ability to utilize more of his army simultaneously. This is a way that he creates havoc in the earth. Matthew 14 vs 33 says, "[33] For God is not the author of confusion, but of peace, as in all churches of the saints." Satan loves for confusion because it has the capacity to shatters man's trust and belief in God.

7
Demonic Concepts of War

²² "Now consider this, you who forget God,
Lest I tear *you* in pieces,
And *there be* none to deliver:
²³ Whoever offers praise glorifies Me;
And to him who orders *his* conduct *aright*
I will show the salvation of God."

Psalm 50

There are times when the enemy will not focus his attention on a community. He will release small agents within his army to target an individual or a person. It is not outside of the ordinary to find families suffering from conflict with the enemy. Generational curses plague many families. They can manifest themselves in behavior patterns, sicknesses, diseases, economic challenges, family disparities, and more. Satan can tailor an attack specialize for a particular family. When a family is going through this type of challenge, they can feel as though they have been abandoned by God. Even though, it is not the truth, the enemy does things to that family intentionally to get them to stop looking for hope in Jesus Christ.

When Satan was permitted to attack Job, his life suffered great things and people around him could not understand what was happening to his life. The enemy believes that personal and direct attacks on individuals will cause them to stop looking for God in their situation. It is the plan of the enemy for people to lose hope in God when things are not changing positively in their timing. Proverbs 13 vs 12 says, "Hope deferred maketh the heart sick: but when the desire cometh, it is a tree of life." There are several occasions in scripture where the enemy tried to leverage their situations in his favor by a delay of time.

The enemy uses the manipulation of time as a weapon against the believer. He will exaggerate time, create delays, or cause time to move swiftly by creating chaos. The person that is waiting on the manifestation of God becomes entrapped by things that hinder their time, they can become frustrated and stop believing God. An example of time becoming exaggerated, and the enemy leveraging the situation is found in the story of Jesus walking on water. In Matthew's account of the story, Jesus commanded His disciples to go to the other side. Jesus was on the mountain praying when they were crossing the sea to the other side. While they were crossing, they encountered a storm that hindered their progress. When the enemy attempts to exaggerate time, he will create a moment of chaos to distract you from moving forward.

John 10 vs 10 says, "The thief does not come except to steal, and to kill, and to destroy. I have come that they may have life, and that they may have it more abundantly." The enemy specializes in mastering these attributes: stealing, killing, and destroying. Because Satan diversifies his agenda throughout his military force, it is difficult for many people to recognize when the enemy is stealing time and detaining their purpose. In the bible story previously mentioned, it is common to pay attention to Jesus' walking on water to save his disciples. However, there are some gems to discover out of the story that will help to understand the nature of Satan's infantry better. Derek Prince says that Satan is a life-taker and tries to intently steal our blessings; Satan is a murderer who purposes himself to destroy our soul and disconnect us eternally from the promise of God.[1] Satan will attempt to stop your momentum by infecting your obedience. The disciples were being obedient to the command that Jesus gave them. The storm that they encountered can be perceived as a natural storm in some context. However, storms that the enemy creates in the lives of mankind are associated with man's willingness to obey the voice of God. It frustrates the enemy when a person can commit their "will" to the purpose and voice of God. The storm that the disciples encountered ignited fear and stopped their movement immediately.

Jesus was on the mountain praying when he heard his disciples in distress. Amazingly, when Jesus appears on the water, the disciples perceived Him to be a ghost. However, they failed to realize that the storm that they had encountered was no longer present and active. The enemy understands, people who are committed to the "will of God" are not easily persuaded. Therefore, he uses tactics that are designed to stop the believer and create anxiety that will stop them from progress. So, in reflection to this story. When Jesus gave the command to go to the other side, the travel time was already calculated. By the disciples not arriving on time, it could have possibly delayed the promise or manifestation of God. Focus is required when the enemy has launched an attack against a person's time.

Satan is frustrated most by the obedience of mankind towards God. Delaying time is one of the most utilized concepts in spiritual battles that the devil uses against the believer. When he is enforcing his agenda towards you directly and being intentional about your self-destruction, he will continue to use time. Learning to resist the devil can be a sign of declaring war against the enemy. James 4 vs 7 says, "Submit yourselves therefore to God. Resist the devil, and he will flee from you." Resistance makes a statement against the enemy's attacks. He does not like human resistance. Therefore, when we resist the devil, he can intensify his approach in the battle by changing his war concept.

God's Glory	Satan's Frustration
• Ensures your faith.	• You will be able to discern between the real voice of God and an impersonated voice of God.
• Not bound to the weaknesses of your flesh.	• You will be able to discern the motives of the situation.
• Validate your righteousness in him (God).	• You are not vulnerable to him (Satan).
• Affirm and strengthen your recognition and hearing of God's Voice.	• You gain strength to encourage others that were victims of him and convince them to pursue God.
• Enable you to walk in VICTORY.	• You become his enemy and not his Prey.

When the enemy is enraged, he can employ a guerrilla warfare concept in spiritual warfare. Traditionally, guerilla warfare is carried out by a military unit operating in a small team designed to undermine the enemy. In spiritual battles, guerilla warfare is carried out by demonic angels who are assigned to produce repetitive cycles or extreme challenges in the life of a person. This tactic is instrumental in challenging a person's faith. The demonic angels that are assigned to engage in these kind of war tactics will undermine the individual's religious position.

In the gospel of Mark chapter 5, there is a story about Jairus request of Jesus to go to his house because of his sick daughter. Uniquely, after Jairus made the request of Jesus, as they were in route to his home, Jesus encounter the woman with the issue of blood. In lieu of Jairus daughter being ill until the point of death. We can see how in his case; the enemy was exaggerating the time of his need to induce discouragement and disbelief in the heart of Jairus about his need being impacted by Jesus. The woman with the issue blood never intended for Jesus to stop in his tracks to attend to her issue. However, it is important to zero in on the guerilla warfare concept that was initiated against Jairus request.

The woman has a need, but her need is not a distraction or deterrent to attend to Jairus need. During this time, a certain ruler from the synagogue told Jairus to end his petition of his Jesus because his daughter is dead.

> "³⁵ While he yet spake, there came from the ruler of the synagogue's house certain which said, Thy daughter is dead: why troublest thou the Master any further? ³⁶ As soon as Jesus heard the word that was spoken, he saith unto the ruler of the synagogue, Be not afraid, only believe. ³⁷ And he suffered no man to follow him, save Peter, and James, and John the brother of James. ³⁸ And he cometh to the house of the ruler of the synagogue, and seeth the tumult, and them that wept and wailed greatly. ³⁹ And when he was come in, he saith unto them, Why make ye this ado, and weep? the damsel is not dead, but sleepeth. ⁴⁰ And they laughed him to scorn. But when he had put them all out, he taketh the father and the mother of the damsel, and them that were with him, and entereth in where the damsel was lying. ⁴¹ And he took the damsel by the hand, and said unto her, Talitha cumi; which is, being interpreted, Damsel, I say unto thee, arise." Mark 5: 35-41 KJV

In verse 35, the guerilla warfare tactic would be intended to create doubt in the man's heart. When the ruler from synagogue imposes his disposition, the enemy initially super imposed his agenda against the man's request for Jesus to come to his home. The enemy uses this tactic against believers today. Satan knows that the average believer does not have stamina or endurance in spiritual battles. If trouble lasts long enough, many people will give up on God. In this case with Jairus, the weapon of choice used in this guerilla tactic is the implementation of doubt.

James 1 vs 6 says, "⁶ But let him ask in faith, nothing wavering. For he that wavereth is like a wave of the sea driven with the wind and tossed." In other passages of scripture, we can see how the enemy uses time delay against the request of believer. He understands that when this weapon is engaged, that the believer can cancel their petition that is present before God because of the doubt that has manifested in their heart. In the story with Jairus, we see the response of a certain ruler from the synagogue informing him to stop his request of the father. However, when Jairus initiated his request for Jesus to come to his home, the situation with his daughter was already a hopeless situation. In as much, this is the purpose of why Jairus travelled to request Jesus to come to his home.

It is common in guerilla warfare for the enemy to use someone that is close to you to initiate doubt, fear, and skepticism in the heart of the believer. There are times when prayer partners and loved one's are waiting on the manifestation of God regarding a situation in your life, but His delay to manifesting the promise in your situation can frustrate them. Their frustration about the delay in your life can force you to be interrogated by familiar people. This is to steal a person's dream. If a person has enough people asking him about the same thing long enough, they can abandon their hope and trust in God. Frank and Ida Mae Hammond say, "Satan has a method---a settled plan---to conquer each one of us, along with our family, church community and nation. God has provided armor for our protection and weapons for offensive warfare."[2] Traditional guerilla warfare can encompass hand to hand combat. Therefore, Satan would use people close to you to activate doubt in your heart about God's ability in certain situations.

Matthew 18 vs 19-20 say, "[19] Again I say unto you, that if two of you shall agree on earth as touching anything that they shall ask, it shall be done for them of my Father which is in heaven. [20] For where two or three are gathered together in my name, there am I in the midst of them." Satan knows the power of agreement in the kingdom. Guerilla warfare is used instrumentally to disrupt agreement and dismantle a person's trust in God. Therefore, when we examine the story with Jairus, Jesus is intentional about putting everyone outside of the home upon his arrival to fulfill the request of Jairus concerning his daughter.

There is another bible story where guerilla warfare is implemented by the enemy. When placing the effects of the enemy in context, you must always remember in many cases the people that are challenging an idea or position are not "the devil." However, anyone can be used by "the devil" to get his agenda passed. In the story of Mary, Martha, and Lazarus; we can see how the enemy uses delay to infiltrate the heart of mankind to lose hope in Jesus Christ.

In John 11, the story of Lazarus resurrection is a hallmark of Christian faith. However, in this story, when Lazarus was sick, Mary and Martha sent word to Jesus to come to the need of Lazarus. When Jesus received the word, the bible says that he intentionally stayed in the same place two more days. Within the two-day period, Lazarus was dead and entombed. The way that guerilla warfare is demonstrated in this story is by the lack of belief, trust, and expectation of Mary, Martha, and others who lost hope in His ability because of the delay of His coming. Therefore, when Jesus showed up at the home, everyone had lost hope in his ability to help Lazarus because of His delay and Lazarus condition. Satan knows that humanity will quantify their expectation in Christ based on logic and reason. In as much, when Jesus is present for Lazarus, no one is able to comprehend why Jesus wants to go to the tomb to see Lazarus. In their logic and reason, Lazarus body should have started decaying, which would have made it an unnecessary, unethical, and unreasonable request for Jesus to go to the tomb.

In guerilla warfare, the enemy diffuses hope, provoke doubt, and initiates fear because it can potentially unstable the heart of a weakened believer. This warfare tactic can also be employed by the enemy when he uses procrastination against the believer. In Matthew 25, the story of the ten virgins and their conversation with the bridegroom demonstrates this guerilla warfare tactic in this story. As Jesus tells the story, there are ten virgins and all of them were given the same instructions, however, only five of them followed the instructions given. Guerilla warfare is a tactic that the enemy uses to cause people to procrastinate based on their own fear and perception. All ten virgins heard the same instructions; they also had access to the resource to fulfill the instructions. However, five of them procrastinated severely. Therefore, when the bridegroom appeared, five of them where not ready to meet him. Because they waited, the bridegroom appeared at midnight, and they did not have any oil in the lamp to guide them on their path. The intensity of the story is when those who were lacking oil requested of those who possessed oil to share with them.

It is important to note that when the enemy is employing guerilla warfare, one of the outcomes of this tactic of war is to create internal conflict. Internal conflict within any system can be like a person activating a grenade in the presence of a platoon. Conflict that happens from within can create distrust and disharmony. Satan uses this to contradict the principle in Christianity, that men should love their neighbor. Guerilla warfare is for the intent of the body of Christ to be drawn together, it is designed for it to remain divided. Mark 3 vs 24 says, "And if a kingdom be divided against itself, that kingdom cannot stand." Satan knows that the Kingdom of God was established in the principle of unification. Heaven remains unified because God is unified with himself. Guerilla warfare is purposed to break that harmony and unification in the heavens. That is why it is important for Satan to utilize these kinds of techniques to create disruption within the body of Christ.

Many communities, families, and organizations have been affected by guerilla warfare. The effect of these battles has caused people to stop communicating, being present for one another, and operating in abandonment towards one another. Adrian Rogers says, "God establishes earthly authorities, but God does not give Kingdom Authority to rebels. As we have repeatedly discovered, we can never be over those things God has put under us until we are under those things that he has set over us."[3] In order to override, overpower, and overthrow the personal attack of the enemy, courage and vulnerability in God must be present.

To counter act the enemy in this kind of warfare, one must operate in forgiveness, love, and resilience. Guerilla warfare from the devil's perspective is not to remain a spiritual battle only. This war tactic is designed to integrate social, racial, economic, and political agendas against mankind. This creates further confusion in communities. Any place where confusion is rampant, disharmony and disunity will be present. Practicing forgiveness reiterates God's love for all men. When you demonstrate this love, it upsets the enemy because there are certain degrees of the love that will be attributed to people who have a strong moral order. John 13 vs 35 says, "By this shall all men know that ye are my disciples, if ye have love one to another."

It remains his agenda to create dissention and use it to disenfranchise people. Thomas Sowell says, "In the real world, however, disparities in outcomes have been common in things extending far beyond socioeconomic differences."[4] Whether the war is army against army, race against race, class against class, or academic differences, the enemy desires to keep people frustrated and lacking trust with each other. Therefore, Satan uses several strategies intertwined with his concept of war to continue terrorizing people, families, and communities.

8
Strategies of War

⁴ The LORD *is* in His holy temple,
The LORD's throne *is* in heaven;
His eyes behold,
His eyelids test the sons of men.
⁵ The LORD tests the righteous,
But the wicked and the one who loves violence His soul hates.
⁶ Upon the wicked He will rain coals;
Fire and brimstone and a burning wind
Shall be the portion of their cup.

⁷ For the LORD *is* righteous,
He loves righteousness;
His countenance beholds the upright

Psalm 11

Satan is the ultimate war strategist. He wars against the heavens but creates dualism between angelic beings and humans. The kingdom of darkness intensifies its offensive and defensive plan by complicated life with strategies of war. Satan knows the body of mankind is more prone to fighting each other directly rather than understanding his indirect involvement in the battle.

It is easy for people to unleash a verbal assault or attack a person's character rather than admit their own inconsistencies or misunderstandings. A person's need to be right can be driven by hidden struggles from within; therefore, the devil does not desire for mankind to have a sense of self-discovery. In most cases, men are more concerned about what they can possess next that they fail at examining themselves for inner weaknesses or discrepancies that should be address. Going through life and not addressing these areas cannot be hidden by good deeds. Paul says in Romans 7 vs 18-19, "[18] For I know that in me (that is, in my flesh,) dwelleth no good thing: for to will is present with me; but how to perform that which is good I find not. [19] For the good that I would I do not: but the evil which I would not, that I do." Because of the innate nature of man to be evil, the devil attempts to penetrate man's desire, his will, and worldview.

Intruding against man's will is Satan's purpose. By doing so, he can dominate areas of the earth and keep his strongholds in place for his agenda. Thomas Aquinas says, "Evil taken generally is a natural corruption of measure, form, and order taken generally. But the evil of punishment befalls the very one who acts, and the evil of moral wrong as such befalls the very action."[1] Our understanding of evil causes man to limit the demonstration of evil being an attribute of human corruption. However, on ground zero of spiritual battles, it must be acknowledged, the Devil is at the root of such causes. Consequently, he utilizes his army to its full capacity. Through his kingdom of darkness, he issues deployments, orders, commands, and wages war in areas where he is desire to control or keep control.

There are several strategies of war that is used in traditional forms of war in the earth. Examining Satan's ability to attack, ambush, and terrorize people, some of these strategies can be contrasted with spiritual battles. The contrast of these concepts can provide clarity on various ways the enemy continues to perpetuate his agenda.

Robert Greene talks about the *33 Strategies of War* in his book. These strategies will provide a deeper understanding for those engaging in spiritual battles with the enemy. Understanding various ways that the enemy can strategically continue to perpetuate his agenda will provide intel for believers. This will enable believers to be proactive and develop counter responses to his intentions. 1 Peter 5 vs 8 says, "Be sober, be vigilant; because your adversary the devil, as a roaring lion, walketh about, seeking whom he may devour."

Satanic Strategies of War

The Grand Strategy

> "The grand strategy is the art of look beyond the battle and calculating ahead. It requires that you focus on your ultimate goal and plot to reach it. Let others get caught up in the twists and turns of the battle, relishing their little victories."[2]

The grand strategy of the devil is to ultimately defy the belief of the believer on the earth while enlarging his kingdom. The purpose of enlarging his kingdom is to strengthen his stronghold on the earth as the *Prince of the Air*. Satan knows that he is a defeated foe, however, his agenda is connected to the perpetual fall of man. Therefore, he is not moved by the testimony of the believer.

Testimonies are for other believers to remain encouraged about God's promise and guarantee to be present with his children. Psalm 91 vs 4 says, "He shall cover thee with his feathers, and under his wings shalt thou trust: his truth shall be thy shield and buckler." The enemy tries to calculate the tolerance of the believer. Consequently, he does what he can to make the believers testimony become null and void.

He attempts to accomplish this with premature deaths, illness, and other things to keep the persons back pressed against the wall of life. His grand strategy encompasses hindering a person from maximizing their potential. There are many people who refuse to walk in their full potential because of the fear they possess. No matter what a person accomplishes in life, the enemy does not lose focus on his agenda. The ultimate way to defeat *the grand strategy* of the enemy is to resist him. Adrian Rogers says, "Satan is a consummate liar, and his is spiritually wicked, brilliantly stupid, and hideously beautiful. He wants to pull the veil of darkness over his activities."[3] Placing a veil over his motives helps him to leverage his agenda.

So, we must remain in the recommended posture suggest by Jude. Jude 1 vs 3 says, "Beloved, when I gave all diligence to write unto you of the common salvation, it was needful for me to write unto you, and exhort you that ye should earnestly contend for the faith which was once delivered unto the saints." Resisting the devil is a counterattack against his plot.

I remember being in the hospital with COVID-19. On the second night, I had a visitation by the spirit of death. I was in a two-patient room. When the spirit of death entered the room, my hospital roommate was becoming nonresponsive. Immediately, the nurse called for the emergency response team on the floor. While the team was on the other side of the curtain attending to me roommate, I was in my bed losing my breath. As I was laying there unable to speak, I stretched my hand and began praying for my roommate in the spirit. As I prayed, things begin to change for him, and oxygen entered my lungs giving me the ability to breathe. I prayed for him, not intentionally desiring to see a miracle; as I prayed for him, I was telling God that his children did not need to experience the death of the loved one during this season. However, I was not able to understand *the grand strategy* of the enemy until the next morning.

On the surface, it looked like the enemy's plan was to allow me to experience a premature death. However, it was much more detailed than what I was thinking. When I awakened the morning after our visit of the spirit of death, God ministered to my heart. He told me that the enemy's plan was to have my life expire at the same age and in the same manner of my father, the later Rev. Roosevelt Ethridge, Sr. If the enemy would have had his way, my son would have been around the age I was when my father's life expired. Also, the enemy was planning to cause ethe same effects to my ministry that he caused to my father's ministry. The point is that the enemy does not look at our future as much as it is true that he studies our behavior, patterns, and responses.

The grand strategy is designed to get the believer fighting the battle on his terms. The believer should never engage a spiritual battle on the terms of the enemy. His grand strategy is to use manipulation and deceit to override the person's trust in God. Always, remember God's strategy for mankind always trump the enemy's plan. Galatians 6 vs 9 says, "And let us not be weary in well doing: for in due season we shall reap, if we faint not."

The Death-Ground Strategy

> "You are your own worst enemy. You waste precious time dreaming of the future instead of engaging in the present. Cut your ties to the past; enter unknown territory. Place yourself on "death ground," where your back is against the wall and you have to fight like hell to get out alive."[4]

The *death-ground strategy* is a strategy that the enemy uses to defeat the believer through their own self-destruction. This strategy is designed to cause the person to live in condemnation. Romans 8 vs 1 says, "There is therefore now no condemnation to them which are in Christ Jesus, who walk not after the flesh, but after the Spirit" The purpose of this strategy is trap the person with inner battles and struggles. The struggles are not always opposing forces like alcohol, infidelity, manipulation, etc. Satan knows that the kingdom of God is established based on unity and relationship. This strategy is used against strong willed people in most cases. They can be gifted and anointed but alone. They struggle with connecting and remaining connected. The struggle to survive in this case does not suggest that people are not financial capable of carrying for themselves, neither does it suggest that a person lacks competency. The goal of this is type of strategy is to cause a person to live life unhappily.

The enemy knows that a person who lives with limitations will never maximize their potential. Also, when a person lives on the island by themselves, they are less likely to explore building relationships that are productive. The *death-ground strategy* is used through offense, negative criticism, and unforgiveness. When people feel threatened or trapped by fear, they are more likely to abandoned relationships or abort commitments. Because of redemption and the atonement of Christ, Satan understands the power of forgiveness, therefore he intently uses his army to employ strategies that will cause people to disassociate themselves with each other.

Organizational Team Warfare

> "You may have brilliant ideas, you may be able to invent unbeatable strategies---but if the group that you lead, and that you depend on to execute your plans, is unresponsive and uncreative, and its members always put their personal agendas first, your ideas will mean nothing. You must learn the lesson of war: it is the structure of the army---the chain of command and the relationship of the parts to the whole---that will give your strategies force. The primary goal in war is to build speed and mobility into the very structure of your army."[5]

The Kingdom of God was established on the principle of teams. In Mark chapter 6, Jesus sends out His disciples two by two. He gave them power over unclean spirits and powers of darkness. At the beginning of his ministry, he draws twelve men to follow him. When he activates the church of Acts, there were 120 disciples waiting in the *Upper Room*. The book of Revelation chapter 4, John talks about the twenty-four elders bowing down and crying Holy. Because the enemy understands the power of agreement, he challenges visionary's with establishing teams and units.

Every visionary that is carrying an assignment with God sometimes experiences a challenge with establishing teams. The challenge is because the enemy understands if people work together in the earth realm that progress can take place against any level of opposition. Therefore, the devil strategically fights teamwork. Keeping people frustrated and annoyed can cause a system to become stagnated. Bruce P. Powers says that there are 6 stages to the life cycle of a church. The 6 stages of the life cycle are: 1. Birth, 2. Development, 3. Peak, 4. Plateau, 5. Decline, 6. Struggle for Survival.[6] Satan fights against organization by camouflaging his motives causing people to fight each other directly, thereby creating hindrances and complacency.

When Israel was in Egypt, first, they prospered because of Joseph's favor with Pharaoh. However, when the leadership and administration of Egypt changed and the new Pharaoh did not know Joseph, Israel was placed in 400 years of hardship, social, and economic oppression. Satan works to stop the progress of the kingdom and impact the wellness of the God's people because he does not want organizations to flourish, grow, or become as support to people, communities, or the world.

The Command-And-Control Strategy

> "The problem in leading any group is that people inevitably have their own agendas. You have to create a chain of command in which they do not feel constrained by your influence yet follow your lead. Create a sense of participation, but do not fall into groupthink---the irrationality of collective decision making."[7]

There are many leaders who encounter the spirit of sabotage when trying to implement a chain of command and demonstrate control of the vision. This spirit of sabotage can cause teams to be restricted to the faithful use of only a few committed people. The commitment of a few people can become scrutinized by the corporate body. The enemy will use persuasion, deception, and critique against visionary leaders to sabotage the impact of the vision.

Satan knows if there is no agreement among men, then there will be little to no progress of the vision. Amos 3 vs 3 raises the question, "Can two walk together, except they be agreed?" It is not ethical to try to progress a vision without the buy-in of others who are part of the vision. When Satan is employing the Command-And-Control strategy, he strategically uses his military force to bring confusion in God's plan for man.

Satan is notorious for trying to manipulate God's original intent for things created or people being used. Adam and Eve were in the garden, the sacred space of God. Satan entered that space and deceived them from God's purpose. He continues to use that strategy today. He will cause people to make decisions in their heart being led by their feelings and not the Spirit of Christ. Satan understands humanism and its impact against the assignment of God.

This strategy is one of Satan's favorite strategies to use because he prides himself on initiating evaluations for Christian leaders to be criticized harshly. In Christ, forgiveness is a common and ethical practice. Forgiveness cannot be practiced if it is coupled with condemnation. Satan is not one who operates in forgiveness. Therefore, he will cause use his army to initiate things that will cause people to live and walk in unforgiveness. Unforgiveness is the weapon of choice and this strategy is being implemented throughout the earth. When this strategy is in effect, usually unforgiveness is applied towards the visionary leader. The goal is to have leaders to walk alone or only with their family. Satan hinders the progress of ministry by causing leaders to spend an unreasonable amount of time resolving conflict rather than making moves of progress.

Morale Strategy

> "The secret to motivating people and maintaining their morale is to get them to think less about themselves and more about the group. Involve them in a cause, a crusade against a hated enemy. Make them see their survival as tied to the success of the army as a whole."[8]

In Satan's army, his motive is to persuade more people to not believe in the community of God. It is common to hear people criticize the church about being holy, supportive, community oriented, giving, etc. However, in most cases, people who criticize are not the ones who do the giving or in some cases help the vision. Satan employs tactics that make people feel as though it is pointless to join a community of believers or commit their lives to a church.

The kingdom of God is designed to embrace the contribution of all men. However, the problem is installed when people begin to measure their contribution by others contribution. If Satan can decrease the morale of people, then their complain and/or disgruntled behavior will become an opposing force against visionary leaders.

In Numbers chapter 20, Moses was instructed by God to speak to the rock for the people to receive water. However, during this time, the people were complaining and antagonizing the visionary leadership of Moses. Moses did not ignore their complaints, which led him to strike the rock instead of speaking to the rock. This demonstrates, when visionary leaders take their eyes off the vision to begin attending to the complaints of people, they can be impacted.

Also, Satan employs this strategy to get people to ignore commitment and to draw other back to a life of loneliness. Satan does not only attack visionary leaders, but his motive is also to ultimately destroy the unification of people who believe in Christ. The morale in Christian communities is elevated by the love that is shown towards mankind. The focus of the love should carry a dual approach. This love should focus on people outside of the ministry but not overlook the need of people within the ministry. Satan creates loopholes in ministry in order to get people distracted by the overall purpose and agenda of God.

The Perfect-Economy Strategy

> "We all have limitations---our energies and skills will make us only so far. You must know your limits and pick your battles carefully. Consider the hidden costs of war: time, lost, political goodwill squandered, and embittered enemy bent on revenge. Sometimes it is better to wait, to undermine your enemies covertly rather than hitting them straight on."[9]

The enemy using this strategy to get people to be on an island by themselves. He will create terror and cause people to lose trust in other people. People become afraid of trusting others with parts of the vision. In addition to that, he will use this strategy to keep communities divided.

He orchestrates his kingdom to cause people to ignited initiatives independent of others. Satan forces people to not work together in hopes of having people use all their resources, time, and energy in rescuing a dying world. The outcome of this strategy is to cause people to remain divided and isolated. Satan knows that the kingdom of God is large, therefore, keeping people isolated is a way that he can continue to move his agenda forward in the earth.

This strategy is used to exhaust the resources and energy of those that are doing the work. At the point when people are exhausted, Satan increase his advancement against them. The Perfect-Economy strategy is subliminal. It is not as forward as other strategies, but it does not lack any potency from any of the other strategies.

The Annihilation Strategy

> "People will use any kind of gap in your defenses to attack you. So, offer no gaps. The secret is to envelop your opponents---create relentless pressure on them from all sides and close off their access to the outside world. As you sense their weaking resolve crush their willpower by tightening the noose."[10]

The enemy loves to break down infrastructure from the inside out. In Christendom, it is common for people to associate infiltration in their army from people that they classify as Judas. It is a misappropriation to place Judas in the category of annihilation when his act of betrayal was necessary for the time of Christ's walk to calvary. Every organization will have a Judas, but the true attribute of Judas is disloyalty and yielding to bribes.

However, the enemy is more subtle in his use of people. He is not interested in the obvious disloyalty of people as much as he is fully invested in placing informants in places that will continue to carry out his agenda. The annihilation strategy encompasses piracy and barbaric natures. Piracy is the act of getting close enough to a system then abandoning the system to go do the exact same thing as the existing system. Barbarians are those people who are not connected to anything but will bully their way into places of prominence and favor.

This strategy is primarily used when Satan is employing his footmen on the ground. He will use people to find out your weaknesses to strategize to plot and those areas to tear down pieces of the infrastructure. Satan despises organization. 1 Corinthians 14 vs 33 says, "For God is not the author through confusion, but of peace, as in all churches of the saints."

Satan also uses this strategy to institute race domination exploits. If he can keep races at war with each other of racial supremacy, then he is able to keep communities isolated and segregated.

Misconception Strategy

> "Since no creature can survive without the ability to see or sense what is going on around it, make it hard for your enemies to know what is going on around them, including what you are doing. Feed their expectations, manufacture a reality to match their desires, and they will fool themselves. Control people's perceptions of reality and you control them."[11]

The enemy terrorizes the life of the believer to confuse them about his involvement in life's crisis. Proverbs 14 vs 12 says, "There is a way which seemeth right unto a man, but the end thereof are the ways of death." The enemy masterminds his attack to impose upon your feelings and emotions. The devil desires for people to make impulsive decisions. Children of God are led by the Spirit of God, not their emotions. The enemy knows that many people will change their direction immediately based on how they feel about a thing, a decision, or situation. He knows that impulsive decisions can lead to death.

There are four ways that he expects people to die: spiritually, physically, financially, and emotionally. Satan knows that if a person feels like they are dying in any of these areas that they will engage a mental battle and they are less likely to produce or move forward in their lives.

The misconception strategy causes people to stand blind and incoherent while being alive in God. Those in Christ walk by faith and not by sight. Satan knows the power of vision; therefore, he fights to block what people see by faith because he prefers the fight to be engaged based on reality or terms that they can see. Unbeknownst to the believer, Satan uses these kinds of battles as bait to draw them in a phase of death.

Communication Strategy

> "Communication is a kind of way, its field of battle the resistant and defensive minds of the people you want to influence. The goal is to penetrate their defenses and occupy their minds. Learn to infiltrate your ideas behind enemy lines, sending messages through little details, luring people into coming to the conclusions you desire and into thinking they've gotten there by themselves."[12]

The first thing that the enemy attacks in battle is our communication. It is common for believers to want to hear from God, however, it is difficult to hear clearly when your emotions are in displaced. Also, when a person's thinking is scattered, it is hard for them to focus on the voice of God.

We live in a time of seasons. It is difficult to discern your season when your season has been filled with trauma. The enemy uses military tactics to try to confuse the seasons. If a person loses hope in God, the enemy can manipulate their confidence and impair their communication with God.

The lack of communication can impact the fellowship that a person has with other believers. Satan knows that a person can end up on a mountain of life by themselves. He prefers to fight them one on one. In Matthew 18, Jesus reminds his disciples about the power of agreement. He tells them that is two or three would touch and agree that he would be among them. The devil knows that God responds to those who believe God together, therefore, he strategizes his attack to break communication among believers and with God simultaneously.

The Inner-Front Strategy

> "By infiltrating your opponents; ranks, working from within to bring them down, you give them nothing to see or react against---the ultimate advantage. To take something you want, do not fight those who have it, but rather join them---then either slowly make it your own or wait for the moment to stage a coup d'état."[13]

The enemy has special forces that are trained to penetrate ranks. He penetrates ranks to stop the flow and the order of things. He can use discord to divide people and keep them divided. Satan used various characters to disrupt God's flow among people. Satan does not endorse the move of the assignment of God.

One of his most effective weapons is using people to tear down people. The strategy of the Inner-Front is demonstrated by tearing down the character of a person. A person who is impacted by this strategy usually will undergo character assassination. Satan understands that when a person's character has been assassinated that it takes a season to reestablish their character.

The devil uses inner conflict and family conflict on the same level. The conflict destroys trust and can cause people to abandon relationships, family, and support systems because of unresolved conflict. Also, this strategy will employ narcissistic leadership. Narcissistic leadership can destroy a good team. The enemy does not care about what tactic he uses, his end goal is to stop everyone from flourishing in God.

The inner-front strategy uses the spirit of sabotage and the spirit of abandonment together as weapons. Using this kind of artillery can cause someone to become angry and begin fighting back in their flesh rather than finding their peace in God.

9
Artillery and Weapons Systems for Believers

¹Praise the LORD!

Praise God in His sanctuary;
Praise Him in His mighty firmament!

² Praise Him for His mighty acts;
Praise Him according to His excellent greatness!

Psalm 150

Spiritual battles require artillery. Believers in Christ have more artillery than fasting and praying to engage in battle with the enemy. Through the traditions of the church, the enemy has become accustomed to believers only utilizing these two weapons during war. In 2 Corinthians 10 vs 4-5, Paul says,

> "4 (For the weapons of our warfare are not carnal, but mighty through God to the pulling down of strong holds;) 5 Casting down imaginations, and every high thing that exalteth itself against the knowledge of God, and bringing into captivity every thought to the obedience of Christ;"

It is impossible to be effective against the enemy while being engaged in a spiritual war. The enemy expects every believer to default in the battle and respond in the carnal. However, when facing a spiritual battle, a person should first assess where they are with the spiritual disciplines. In vs 4, Paul says are weapons are not carnal, therefore, you should look towards those non-carnal weapons to combat this enemy. Adrian Rogers says, "Satan will marshal all the forces of hell and the demons of darkness to keep you in ignorance about your Kingdom Authority."[1] Keeping a person ignorant of their kingdom authority will force them alienate their spiritual disciplines.

The spiritual disciplines include prayer, fasting, devotion, study, service, giving, and meditation. Engaging in the spiritual disciplines help to build the stamina and endurance of the Christian soldiers. Because the weapons of the believer are not carnal, each believer must be able to recognize when they need new artillery in their battles. Ephesians chapter 6 only mentions one weapon as it talks about the amor of God. The only weapon that it mentions is the "sword of truth." However, there are more weapons that can be used in battle with the enemy. Dereck Prince says, "...Christ has committed to His Church two special responsibilities. The first is to restrain Satan's purposes on earth until God's purpose of grace have been fulfilled. --- The second responsibility that Christ has committed to His followers is to cast down Satan's kingdom from the heavenlies."[2]

Satan knows that believers have the power to resist him. Moreover, he knows that many believers never tap into their inner strength to overthrow him. Many times, this is because there is a lack of understanding about the roles of God and the roles of the Holy Spirit. The role of God is to release unmerited grace in the earth and the role of the Holy Spirit is to operate as an intermediary and guide for the believer in the earth. The enemy fights to disrupt that communication between God and man through the work of the Holy Spirit. When Satan commissions his powers of darkness to attack an individual personally, he is anticipating that the person will beak under pressure. Adrian Rogers says, "When we submit to a godless government, a bad boss, or a mean mate, we are really submitting to God; he honors that and invest in us Kingdom Authority."[3]

Defeating the enemy requires for you to understand the power that was given to you upon creation. In Psalm 8 it refers to God creating man a little lower than the angels. But man has more authority than the angels because of the work of the cross. You cannot afford to allow demonic angels to pressure you outside of the perfect will of God. Galatians 6 vs 9 says, "And let us not be weary in well doing: for in due season we shall reap, if we faint not." Remaining patient in the battle can become challenging but remain encouraged because God remains faithful.

Sometimes Satan is fighting against your commitment in God. He does not like for anyone to have total trust in God. Therefore, he employs tactics that are designed to frustrate the believer's peace. He does not mind anyone finding out the names of demons, demonic spirits or more, he just does not want anyone to remain faithful to God.

Romans 8 vs 35-37 says, "[35] Who shall separate us from the love of Christ? shall tribulation, or distress, or persecution, or famine, or nakedness, or peril, or sword? [36] As it is written, For thy sake we are killed all the day long; we are accounted as sheep for the slaughter. [37] Nay, in all these things we are more than conquerors through him that loved us." There will be times in life that feels like there is no way out of the situation. However, God is not expecting his children to see their way out of situations, he expects his children to see him in every situation. Romans 8 implies that there will be things that will cause us to feel like we are being separated from the Father.

Just because the enemy places a challenge in a person's life or a community does not mean that God has forsaken them in the situation. The enemy's job is to make a person embrace a mind of hopelessness. Therefore, believers must remain dualistic in their approach to God. Every believer must have a vertical relationship with God and a horizontal relationship with mankind. Satan throws everything he can at mankind to destroy their knowledge of Christ. It is important to love your neighbor as yourself.

Loving mankind undermines the enemy's agenda. People who live in forgiveness and harmony with each other will frustrate the purpose of enemy. Practicing agape love demonstrates God's love for mankind. It is important to note that the enemy does not have a weapon that can destroy the effects of love. Even when people experience abandonment or disloyalty, it is impossible to destroy the manifestation of love once a person has experienced this kind of love. To display love a believer must be selfless. Selfless love resembles the heart of a giver.

Luke 6 vs 38 says, "Give, and it shall be given unto you; good measure, pressed down, and shaken together, and running over, shall men give into your bosom. For with the same measure that ye mete withal it shall be measured to you again." The kingdom of God is built on reciprocation. Satan knows the law of reciprocity. His kingdom is organized to prohibit the law of reciprocity from being a benefit of the God's children. Luke provides creditability about the law of reciprocity. If the enemy can hinder this law from manifesting in the life of a believer, it could increase the chances of a person no longer believing in God's resurrection power.

Satan can be defeated in the earth when believers guard their five senses. These senses can be used as gateways to stop a person from experiencing God in his fulness. You must guard your: eyes, smell, taste, touch, and hearing. The enemy can initiate a battle with a person or community by engaging these five senses. Satan is not concerned about religion; his main concern is about commitment.

Satan does not want anyone to walk in virtue and stand in conviction. Through the power of forgiveness, God's compassion towards mankind permits him to receive them back into his arms. The reason that Satan engages in spiritual battles is to stop believers from embracing the grace of God. He knows that if a person can embrace the grace of God, then redemption is near for them. Therefore, he tries to torment them then with disappoint and depression.

It is not uncommon for a believer to have faith in God and experience depression in life. When we are void of fresh encounters with God, daily devotion with the father then Satan knows that it is only a matter of time before life will become a burden for the believer.

Believers must learn to fortify themselves. One of the most effective ways to fortify yourself is to embrace the four cardinal virtues. The four virtues are: prudence, justice, fortitude, temperance. Possessing these virtues are signs of one's spiritual growth and maturity. We do not gain these virtues automatically because of aging. Josef Pieper, a twentieth-century philosopher knew the importance of these four virtues.

"Virtue is a "perfected ability" of man as spiritual person; and justice, fortitude, and temperance, as "abilities" of the whole man, achieve their "perfection" only when they are founded upon prudence, that is to say upon the perfected ability to make right decisions."[4] The devils knows that we are perfected in Christ, therefore, his agenda includes showing the imperfections of Christians. Highlighted Christian imperfections will lessen the chance of their lives being seen as an example by others. Prudence is a contaminating virtue. Meaning, because of this virtue's potency, the enemy knows the outcome of people who encounter prudent people.

Jesus was on the cross and encountered two individuals that experienced his prudence. The first encounter was the thief that was suffering capital punishment who asked to be remembered when Jesus came into his own. The second was the soldier who identified in the divinity of Christ after piercing him in the side. Understanding the tactics of Satan, he is more effective when isolating the victim and cutting them off from the world.

Justice is an explosive virtue. Satan does not like when people stand up for justice. People who stand up for justice directly stands against injustice. The enemy creates resistance but despises those who resist him. When a person stands up for justice, they are now demonstrating the divine strength that has been granted to them to stand. Josef Pieper says, "Justice reaches beyond the individual subject, because in a certain sense it is itself the bonum alteritus, the "good of another."" Believers position in justice is not only recognized by the things they advocate for or against in the earth. The most offensive stance against the devil is a stance of faith in God. Standing with God causes the devil to become directly offended by this stance. Therefore, fortitude must become part of the Christian position in resisting the devil.

Fortitude can be seen as a wall. This imaginary wall makes it hard for the devil to penetrate. He strategically tries to find ways to penetrate walls that are fortified. Some of the tactics that he uses to break these ranks subliminally are transitions, conflicts, desire, etc. The tactics are not designed to appear as something wrong or difficult, however, the outcome of these decisions when they are demonically induced can produce outcomes that lead to a dead-end. Josef Pieper says, "Prudence and justice precede fortitude. And that means, categorically: without prudence, without justice, there is no fortitude; only he who is just and prudent can also be brave;"[6] It requires courage to be brave in the face of the enemy. Being brave in God requires us to remain obedient to Him. There are times when God will prompt you to run towards things that are bigger than you. The devil is the father of fear and God is the father of faith.

Temperance is necessary to remain faithful. Without temperance it would be easy to discard your convictions. The conviction we have in Christ is the driving force behind one's will to remain faithful to Christ in tough times. The devil does not like faithfulness. Even as we are instructed in 2 Timothy chapter 2 to endure hardship. The devil loves to inflict harm and conflict in the life of people. "For temperance not only preserves, but it also defends: indeed, it preserves by defending."[7] Therefore when the devil is ultimately enraged when we are contending for the faith. Contending for the faith is defending what God has already established as His written word. It also means that we believe in the agenda of the kingdom of God when we defend the principles as the truth.

Romans 12 reminds believers to present their bodies as a living sacrifice. Standing with these virtues can aid use in reaching nations. The enemy does not like when we stand together. Standing together ignites disgust in the devil. But nations are waiting for the church to be revealed in each era of time.

10
Kingdom Intelligence

¹Praise the Lord!

Praise, O servants of the Lord,
Praise the name of the Lord!
² Blessed be the name of the Lord
From this time forth and forevermore!
³ From the rising of the sun to its going down
The Lord's name *is* to be praised.

⁴ The Lord *is* high above all nations,
His glory above the heavens.

Psalm 113

Intelligence is very important in winning war. To gain intelligence trust must be formed. Allies must be identified, and trust must continue to be established even when war is in progress. The devil uses all his military force to find out details about communities, people, families, etc. He gathers his intelligence from behavior and emotional responses about people. The intelligence that he gathers gives him leverage to employ direct attacks against people. Satan knows that some people look for spiritual attacks to identify names of his footmen, but they do not possess the strength to endure the attack that will be imposed against them. Therefore, it is important for us to gather intelligence on the devil.

Emotional intelligence is something that we should study and examine. The emotions are frequently attacked and can impact a person's perception. The old saying is correct, if you think of something bad long enough about a person that you will end up seeing what you are looking for in that person. The enemy loves to manipulate the emotions. "Cultural intelligence consists of three aspects, including cognitive, motivational, and behavioral elements."[1] The devil manipulates these three areas in people lives. However, it is possible to use the same three areas to gain intelligence on the devil

You cannot spend time trying to study the image of the devil. You must learn the devil by his character, his ways, and his attributes. You will be able to gain emotional intelligence from the devil through your interaction with people. Take an assessment of people that you interact with, ask yourself, what have I picked up from this person that does not compliment who I am, or what have I picked up that adds value to who I am? As you study people you will be able to pick emotional intelligence about the devil.

Whether it is individual or corporate, gaining emotional intelligence on the devil is key. The sooner that you can detect the emotional war that he creates and why, the sooner you will be able to counter act his movements. Satan's agenda will never change. He has planned to terrorize the earth, while causing people to lose hope in God. In the story of David and Saul, it is evident that David was gaining emotional intelligence about his enemy. David, knowing that Saul was intentional about killing him, refused to take Saul's life because he was assured that Saul was God's choice. Gathering proper intel on the devil can help curve your response when he manifests in the earth.

The devil manipulates the emotional behavior of people through deception. Being deceived by the enemy can cause people to become rebellious and/or belligerent. Discerning of spirits is one of the nine spiritual gifts that are given to us in 2 Corinthians 10. It is imperative to use discernment in detecting the enemy. Ephesians 6 says that we should put on the whole armor of God so that we can stand against the plans of the enemy. A person that is not able to discern the spirit of the enemy are more likely to be impacted by the enemy's mental and emotional games. Frank and Ida Mae Hammond say, "Disturbances in the emotions which persist or recur. Some of the most common disturbances are resentment, hatred, anger, fear, rejection, (feeling unwanted and unloved), self-pity, jealousy, depression, worry, inferiority, and insecurity."[2]

The devil's strategy is to have people living in this confusion, then causing them to not walk in forgiveness. When we are challenged with emotional intelligence, then it is most likely that we will be challenged with cultural intelligence. There is a theory that suggests Sundays are the most segregated day of the week. If we look closely, we could see that the enemy is the mastermind behind the segregation and/or isolation.

Matthew Kim talks about *Cultural Intelligence*, he says that preaching should not be tailored to fit the individual preacher, but the preacher should approach the sermon on the day of delivery to reach everyone that is in the room.[3] The devil can manipulate people by search for comfort in relationship to church instead of community. When the intelligence of the enemy is poorly assessed, it is easy to find a person who has neglected assignments or times of cultivation

Christian ethics helps us to explore ways of gathering intelligence about the enemy. The ethics of Christianity is buried in principles. These principles are extractions of Christian values that causes Christians to stand up and stand out. Gathering the proper intel will cause a person to stand in boldness unapologetically.

Satan does not desire for anyone to stand boldly for Christ. The military structure of Satan is design to attack those who stand boldly. To stand boldly, you must possess the courage to take the criticism but also have the willingness to project the kingdom forward. Having good intelligence on the enemy can give one insight on how to move around the enemy's traps. The devil does not tolerate resistance without a fight. It is important to keep your focus on Christ while engaging in battle.

SELECTED BIBLIOGRAPHY

Amorth, Fr. Gabriele. *An Exorcist Explains the Demonic: The Antics of Satan and His Army of Fallen Angels.* Manchester: Sophia Institute Press, 2016.

Ang, P. Christopher Earley and Soon. *Cutural Intelligence: Individual Interactions Across Cultures.* Stanford: Stanford Business Books, 2003.

Attridge, Harold W. *The HarperCollins Study Bible New Revised Standard Version:Student Edition.* New York: HarperOne, 1989.

Biblesoft, Inc. *Blue Letter Bible.* 2011. https://www.blueletterbible.org/lang/lexicon/lexicon.cfm?Strongs=G3540&t=KJV (accessed March 2, 2021).

Cavanaugh, William T. *Being Consumed: Economics and Christian Desire.* Grand Rapids: William B. Eerdmans Publishing Company, 2008.

Dennis Linn, Sheila Fabricant Linn, Matthew Linn. *Don't Forgive Too Soon: Extending the Two Hands That Heal.* Mahwah: Paulist Press, 1997.

DeYoung, Rebecca Konyndyk. *Glittering Vices: A new Look at the seven deadly sins and their remedies.* Grand Rapids: BrazosPress, 2009.

Greene, Robert. *The 33 Strategies of War.* New York: Penguin Books, 2006.

Hammond, Frank & Ida Mae. *Pigs In The Parlor: A Practical Guide To Deliverance.* Kirkwood: Impact Books Inc, 1973.

Hannah, John. "The Doctrine of Original Sin in Postrevolutionary America." *Bibotheca Sacra 134 no 535*, July-September 1977: 240.

Hopson, Dr. Darlene Powell Hopson and Dr. Derek S. *The Power of Soul: Pathways to Psychological and Spiritual Growth for African Americans.* New York: William Morrow and Company, Inc., 1998.

Kierkegaard, Soren. *The Sickness Unto Death: A Christian Psychological Exposition for Upbuilding and Awakening.* Princeton: Princeton University Press, 1980.

Kim, Matthew. *Preaching with Cultural Intelligence: Understanding the People who Hear our Sermons.* Grand Rapids: Baker Academic Publishing Group, 2017.

Mbiti, John S. *African Religions and Philosophy.* Jordan Hill: Heinemann Educational Publishers, 2006.

Paula A. Price, Ph.D. *The Prophets Dictionary: The Ultimate Guide to Supernatural Wisdom.* New Kensington: Whitaker House, 2006.

Pieper, Josef. *The Four Cardinal Virtues*. Notre Dame: University of Notre Dame Press, 1966.

Powers, Bruce P. *Congregational Leadership and Administration*. Buies Creek: Bruce P Powers, 2014.

Prince, Derek. *Pulling Down Strongholds*. New Kensington: Whitaker House Publishing, 2013.

Robenson, Drs. Jerry & Carol. *Strongmans His Name...What's His Game*. New Kensington: Whitaker House, 1984.

Sawyer, Ralph D. *Sun Tzu: Art of War*. New York: Basic Books, 1994.

Shapiro, Thomas M. *The Hidden Cost of Being African American: How wealth perpetuates inequality*. New York: Oxford Press University, 2004.

Sowell, Thomas. *Discreminiation and Disparities*. New York: Basic Books, 2019.

Stefon, Matt. *Encyclopedia Britannica*. April 7, 2021. https://www.britannica.com/biography/Anton-LaVey (accessed October 20, 2021).

Wiley, Tatha. *Original Sin: Origins, Developments, Contemporary Meanings*. New York: Paulist Press, 2002.

2003.Attridge, Harold W. The HarperCollins Study Bible New Revised Standard Version:Student Edition. New York: HarperOne, 1989.Biblesoft, Inc. Blue Letter Bible. 2011. https://www.blueletterbible.org/lang/lexicon/lexicon.cfm?Strongs=-G3540&t=KJV (accessed March 2, 2021

Notes

Demonic Strategies

1. Saint Augustine
2. Mitchell Reddish
3. C.S Lewis
4. Adrian Rogers
5. Dr. Henry Cloud and Dr. John Townsend
6. Dr. Henry Cloud and Dr. John Townsend
7. Julian Perreira
8. Shirley Vinson
9. Carter G. Woodson Mis-Education of Negro
10. Jeffrey Burton Russell
11. Derek Prince Pulling Down Strongholds
12. Thomas Sowell
13. Ken Wytsma
14. Abhijit V. Banerjee and Esther Duflo

Satan's ID

1. Tony W. Cartledge
2. Strong's Definitions, Blue Letter Bible, s.v. "serpent," accessed March 26, 2021, https://www.blueletterbible.org/lang/lexicon/lexicon.cfm?Strongs=H5175&t=NKJV
3. Harper Collins Bible Dictionary, s.v. "Zoroaster", accessed March 26, 2021, 1248.
4. William T. Cavanaugh
5. Dr. Darlene Powell Hopson and Dr. Derek S. Hopson
6. Rebecca Konyndyk DeYoung
7. Rebecca Konyndyk DeYoung
8. Rebecca Konyndyk DeYoung
9. Rebecca Konyndyk DeYoung
10. Drs. Jerry & Carol Robeson
11. Rebecca Konyndyk De Young
12. Josef Pieper
13. Rebecca Konyndyk DeYoung
14. Rebecca Konyndyk DeYoung
15. Rebecca Konyndyk DeYoung
16. Abhijit V. Banerjee and Esther Duflo
17. Rebecca Konyndyk DeYoung

Devil Strategic Plan

1. Drs. Jerry & Carol Robeson
2. Derek Prince Pulling Down Strongholds
3. Frank & Ida Mae Hammond
4. Shirley Vinson
5. Dennis Linn, Sheila Fabricant Linn, Matthew Linn
6. Thomas M. Shapiro

Satan's Military Organizational Structure

1. Strong's Definitions, Blue Letter Bible, s.v. "prince," accessed October 14, 2021, https://www.blueletterbible.org/lexicon/g758/kjv/tr/0-1/
2. Strong's Definitions, Blue Letter Bible, s.v. "principality," accessed October 14, 2021, https://www.blueletterbible.org/lexicon/g746/kjv/tr/0-1/

Military Infrastructure of the Devil's Kingdom

1. Paul A. Price, Ph.D.
2. Ralph D. Sawyer
3. Matt Stefon
4. Derek Prince Pulling Down Strong Holds
5. Frank & Ida Mae Hammond
6. Fr. Gabriele Amorth

Rules of Engagement

1. Derek Prince Rules of Engagement
2. Strong's Definitions, Blue Letter Bible, s.v. "mind," accessed October 22, 2021, https://www.blueletterbible.org/lexicon/g3563/kjv/tr/0-1/
3. Father Gabriele Amorth
4. Tatha Wiley
5. John Hannah
6. Soren Kierkegaard
7. Father Gabriele Amorth
8. Adrian Rogers

Demonic Concepts of War

1. Derek Prince Spiritual Warfare
2. Frank and Ida Mae Hammond
3. Adrian Rogers

4. Thomas Sowell

Strategies of War

1. Thomas Aquinas
2. Robert Greene
3. Adrian Rogers
4. Robert Greene
5. Robert Greene
6. Bruce P. Powers
7. Robert Greene
8. Robert Greene
9. Robert Greene
10. Robert Greene
11. Robert Greene
12. Robert Greene
13. Robert Greene

Artillery and Weapons Systems for Believers

1. Adrian Rogers
2. Derek Prince
3. Adrian Rogers
4. Josef Pieper
5. Josef Pieper
6. Josef Pieper
7. Josef Pieper

Kingdom Intelligence

1. P. Christopher Early and Soon Ang
2. Frank and Ida Mae Hammond
3. Matthew Kim

Other books from the Roosevelt Ethridge:

The Making of A Prayer Warrior

You Don't Won't a Boaz

The Battle Ground: A historic preview to Spiritual Warfare

AVAILABLE AT WWW.RELIVEGLOBALCORP.COM

www.ingramcontent.com/pod-product-compliance
Lightning Source LLC
Chambersburg PA
CBHW070343010526
44119CB00029B/415/J